Spelling Rules!

Janelle Ho and
Helen Pearson

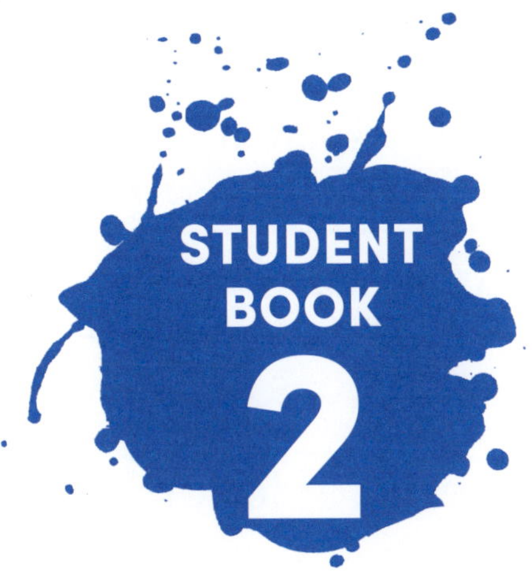

Australian Curriculum Edition

Name: ______________________________

Class: ______________________________

CONTENTS

SLLURP

SLLURP summarises the spelling strategies that you can use to learn new words.

Say	Say the word carefully and slowly to yourself.
Listen	Listen to how each part of the word sounds in sequence.
Look	Look at the patterns of letters in the word and the shape of the word.
Understand	Understand rules, word meanings and word origins.
Remember	Remember all the similar words you can already spell and relate this knowledge to any new word.
Practise	Practise writing the word until it is firmly fixed in your long-term memory.

Scope and Sequence

UNIT	SKILL FOCUS						WORD LIST
	Vowels	Consonants	Letter patterns	Morphology	Homophones/ Homographs	Topic words	
1	digraphs	digraphs and blends					heel, steep, seal, treat, spark, charm, first, third, south, crowd
2	split digraphs: a-e, i-e, o-e, e-e, u-e	blends and digraphs		-ed, -ing: dropping final 'e'			place, scrape, time, unite, slope, whole, complete, squeeze, rule, cure
3	short vowel sounds	blends and digraphs		-ed, -ing: doubling final consonant			beg, scan, clap, strap, swim, begin, block, throb, thud, scrub
4	short y as vowel sound			-y: dropping final 'e', doubling final consonant			lady, carry, sorry, busy, pony, ready, spotty, foggy, furry, chilly
5		ck, medial ck					chicken, bucket, ticket, packet, pocket, jacket, cricket, bracket, backpack, limerick
6	REVISION						
7		silent letters: kn, wr, mb					knee, knife, knock, lamb, thumb, wrong, wrist, listen, castle, often
8	o-e, oa				rode/road/rowed, groan/grown		home, bone, smoke, alone, coat, road, loaf, soap, float, toast
9	ue		ew				new, knew, chew, grew, blew, threw, blue, true, argue, cruel
10			ear, eer		tear, wind, bow; hear/here, dear/deer		fear, hear, tear, clear, spear, weary, appear, deer, peer, cheer, queer
11				re-, un-, dis-			reread, renew, reuse, recycle, undo, untie, unkind, unfair, disagree, disappear
12	REVISION						
13				compound words, plural words			sunhat, gumboot, bedroom, shoelace, toenail, jellyfish, raincoat, hairbrush, newspaper, wheelchair
14				adding -es to words ending in s, x, ss, sh, ch, o			buses, foxes, classes, dresses, wishes, brushes, lunches, branches, potatoes, tomatoes
15				irregular plurals	deer/dear		fish, deer, sheep, mice, feet, teeth, geese, children, women, people
16		st, str, squ			steel/steal		stamp, stew, storm, style, street, strong, stroll, stripe, squeak, square
17		tch		adding -es to words ending in tch	witch/which		itchy, witch, stitch, catch, hatch, watch, fetch, stretch, clutch, kitchen
18	REVISION						
19	oi, ai		oy, ay				annoy, toyshop, join, spoil, noisy, stray, delay, trail, chain, explain
20	ie		ey		piece/peace		chief, thief, field, shield, piece, believe, key, honey, monkey, turkey
21				-es, -ed: changing y to i			babies, ladies, ponies, stories, puppies, cries, carries, worries, hurries, replies
22			aw, oor		draw/drawer, paw/ poor/pour, saw/sore, raw/roar		saw, draw, claw, straw, crawl, yawn, prawn, poor, door, floor
23		spr, scr, spl, thr, shr				seasons of the year	spring, sprawl, screen, scratch, split, splash, shrink, shrill, throw, thread
24	REVISION						
25				contractions			I'll, he's, it's, isn't, can't, don't, doesn't, didn't, won't, we're
26				-ly: changing 'y' to 'i'			sadly, loudly, slowly, nicely, rudely, quickly, quietly, crossly, kindly, happily
27			er, ir	-er, -est: practising spelling rules			fern, serve, person, perfect, stir, shirt, first, dirty, thirsty, birthday
28			ur, or, ear				turn, hurt, burst, nurse, curly, work, worth, learn, earth, search
29				-er, -or		occupations	farmer, leader, baker, teacher, shopper, doctor, actor, visitor, author, sailor
30	REVISION						
31						days of the week	Monday, Tuesday, Wednesday, Thursday, Friday, Saturday, Sunday, today, tomorrow, because
32	ie		igh				lie, pie, tie, high, thigh, right, night, flight, height, weight
33		ld			boulder/bolder		build, world, scold, would, could, should, wouldn't, mouldy, shoulder, boulder
34				compound words with no, any, some, every			no one, nothing, nowhere, somebody, something, anyone, anything, another, everyone, everywhere
35	REVISION						

NOTE TO TEACHERS AND PARENTS

Spelling Rules!

Some students are natural spellers. But the vast majority of students need formal, systematic and sequential instruction about the way spelling works and the strategies they can use to become independent, confident spellers and spelling risk-takers.

The *Spelling Rules!* program is based on sound linguistic and pedagogical theory. It is informed by research into how students of different ages acquire and apply spelling skills, and how those skills move from the working to the long-term memory. The program closely follows the Australian English curriculum. *Australian Curriculum: English* references are provided in the Teacher Resource Books. The program consists of seven student books, fully supported by two Teacher Resource Books.

Each student book contains units of work, with each unit designed to be used over the course of a week. The content of each unit simultaneously develops new skills and reinforces skills from previous units. The introduction of new sounds and letter patterns is logically sequenced and takes into account both frequency of use and complexity. Where appropriate, topic words from other curriculum areas such as mathematics, science and social sciences are included. When spelling rules are introduced, only known sounds and letter patterns are used so that students focus on one skill at a time. Regular revision units enable teachers to assess student progress and reinforce key rules and patterns from previous units.

The *Spelling Rules!* program also incorporates elements of self-assessment. A simple reflection activity allows students to assess their own progress and provides you with a starting point for discussion.

Spelling knowledge

Learning to spell involves developing different kinds of spelling knowledge:

- **Kinaesthetic knowledge** – the physical feeling when saying different sounds and words, and when writing the shapes of letters and words
- **Phonological knowledge** – how a word sounds and the patterns of sounds in words
- **Visual knowledge** – how letters and words look and the visual patterns in words
- **Morphemic knowledge** – the meaning or function of words or parts of words
- **Etymological knowledge** – the origins and history of words and the effect this has on spelling patterns.

Icons used in Student Book 2

The following icons identify the main spelling strategy that students will use to complete an activity.

Say the word. (Kinaesthetic knowledge) These activities ask students to experience how sounds feel in the mouth and jaw. Changing the positions of the jaw, lips and tongue changes the sounds we make. Encourage students to pronounce the sounds and words accurately. If they mispronounce a sound or word, they may misrepresent it in writing.

Listen to the word. (Phonological knowledge) These activities focus on discriminating between different sounds and breaking up words into syllables or individual sound segments (phonemes).

Look at the word. (Visual knowledge) These activities help students to see how the sound is represented using combinations of letters, and to associate this visual pattern with what they are hearing. Students will develop the ability to know when a word does or does not 'look right'.

Understand the word. (Morphemic and etymological knowledge) These activities focus on word meanings, word families, prefixes and suffixes, spelling rules, word origins and so on, which help embed spelling in the long-term memory.

Practise writing the word. (Kinaesthetic knowledge) These activities develop students' awareness of the physical movement involved in writing the word. By practising writing the word a number of times and in different contexts, the spelling becomes embedded in the long-term memory.

This icon highlights useful spelling rules.

This icon tells students that a special clue or hint is provided for an activity. It may be a spelling, grammar or punctuation convention, or a definition of a useful term.

Encourages students to assess their progress across each unit.

Student Book 2

Units of work

Student Book 2 contains 35 weekly units of work. See the **Scope and Sequence chart** on page 3 for more information. Each revision unit gives students an opportunity to self-assess.

Word lists

In *Student Book 2*, each unit (except Revision) has a list of spelling words. The core words in the lists have been chosen to support the learning focus and strategies being taught in the unit.

Spelling lists enable a spelling element to be focused on, and provide sufficient examples to consolidate the teaching point. Topic words come from other curriculum areas, such as mathematics and social sciences. In addition, homophones and words that are easily confused with each other are explained and practised.

SLLURP

Each word list begins with a reminder for students to SLLURP. SLLURP summarises the strategies that will help spelling move from students' working memory to their long-term memory. These strategies are provided on page 2, for easy reference.

Unit at a glance

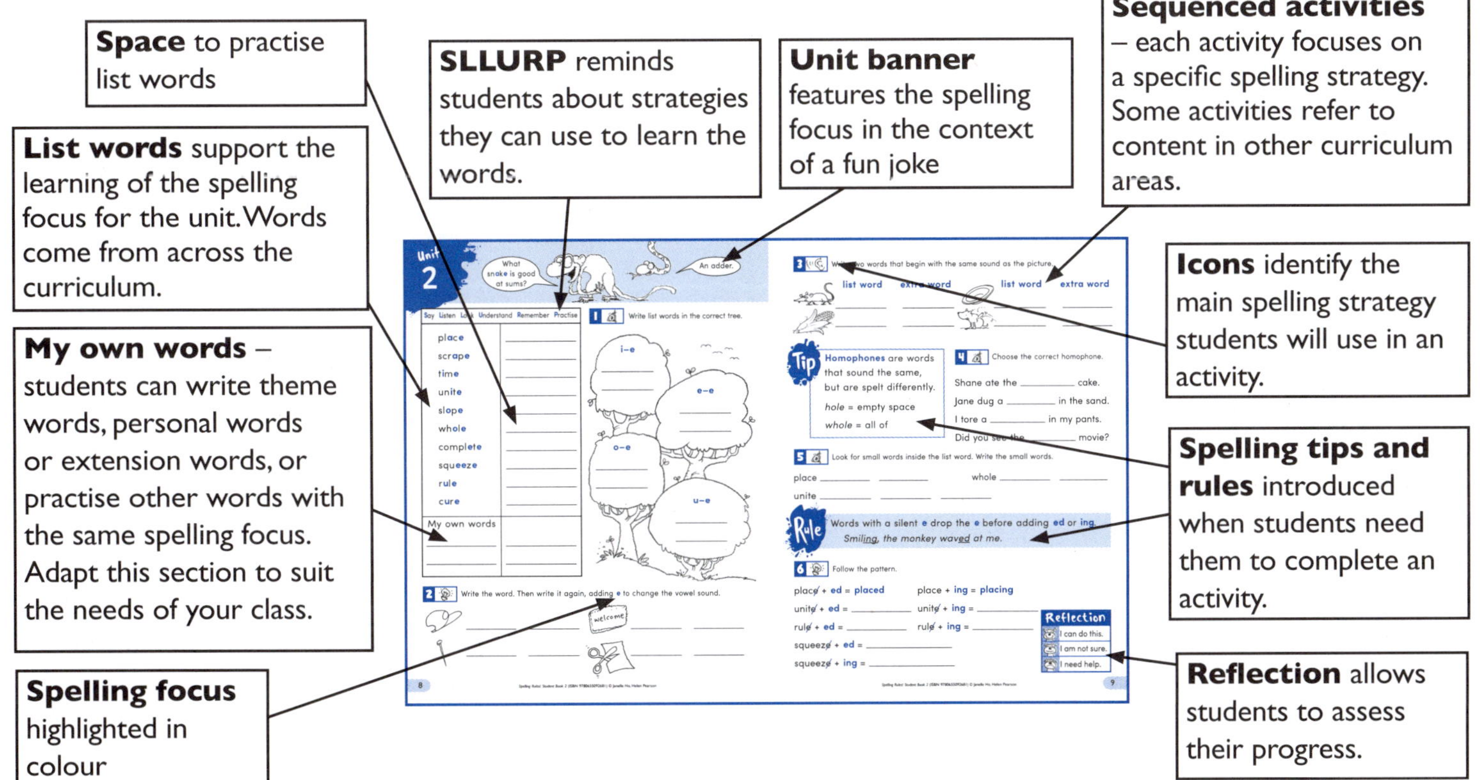

Spelling Rules! Teacher Resource Book F–2

Full teacher support for *Student Book 2* is provided by *Spelling Rules! Teacher Resource Book F–2*. Here you will find valuable background information about spelling development and spelling knowledge, along with practical resources, such as:

- teaching tips for every unit in *Student Book 2*
- extra word lists
- strategies for teaching spelling
- guidelines for assessment and diagnosis of errors
- activities to support struggling spellers
- worthwhile extension for more able spellers.

Unit 1

Say Listen Look Understand Remember Practise	
heel	______
steep	______
seal	______
treat	______
spark	______
charm	______
first	______
third	______
south	______
crowd	______
My own words	
______	______
______	______

1 Write **ee** or **ea**.

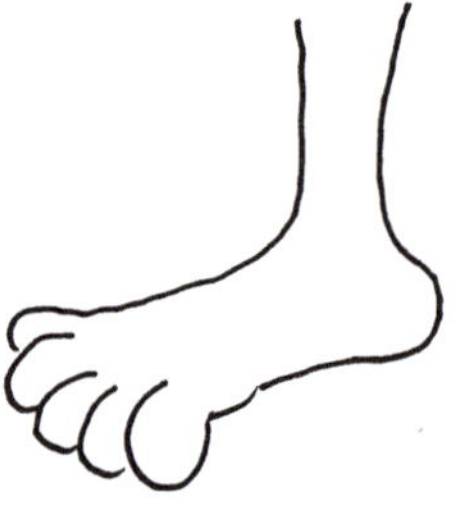

h__ __l

tr__ __

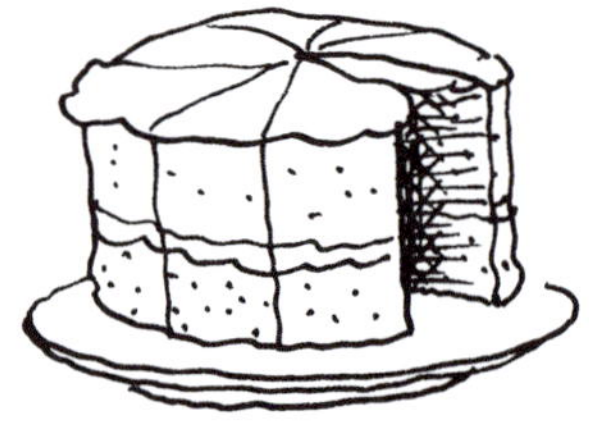

tr__ __t

sp__ __k

sl__ __p

s__ __l

2 Write **ow** or **ou**.

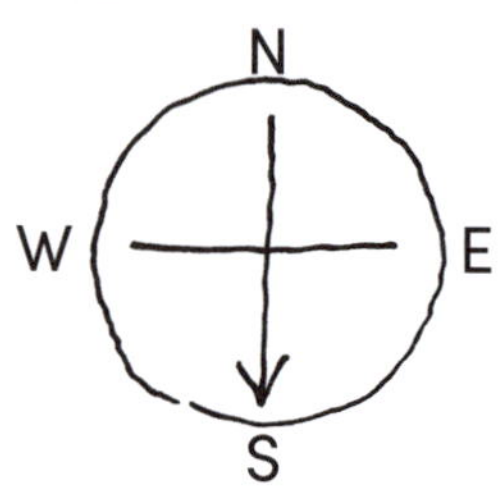

s__ __th

c__ __

cl__ __n

h__ __se

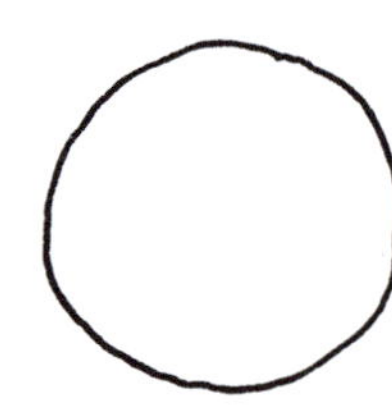

r__ __nd

Say the words. Circle the words that have a different vowel sound.

far	warn	ward	farm
war	barn	yard	charm
star	yarn	hard	warm

What do you notice about all the words you circled? ______________________

Add **s**, **ed** and **ing**.

	add **s**	add **ed**	add **ing**
cheat	______	______	______
start	______	______	______
peel	______	______	______
crowd	______	______	______
firm	______	______	______

Colour the correct word.

The chick | cheeps | cheeped | cheeping | when it saw its mum.

Gramps | fears | feared | fearing | he will fall if he walks too fast.

John is | talks | talked | talking | so softly that his friends cannot hear him.

6 Write a sentence using both words.

first
third

____

____

____

Spelling Rules! Student Book 2 (ISBN 9780655092681) © Janelle Ho, Helen Pearson

Unit 2

Say Listen Look Understand Remember Practise	
place	______
scrape	______
time	______
unite	______
slope	______
whole	______
complete	______
squeeze	______
rule	______
cure	______
My own words	
______	______
______	______

1 Write list words in the correct tree.

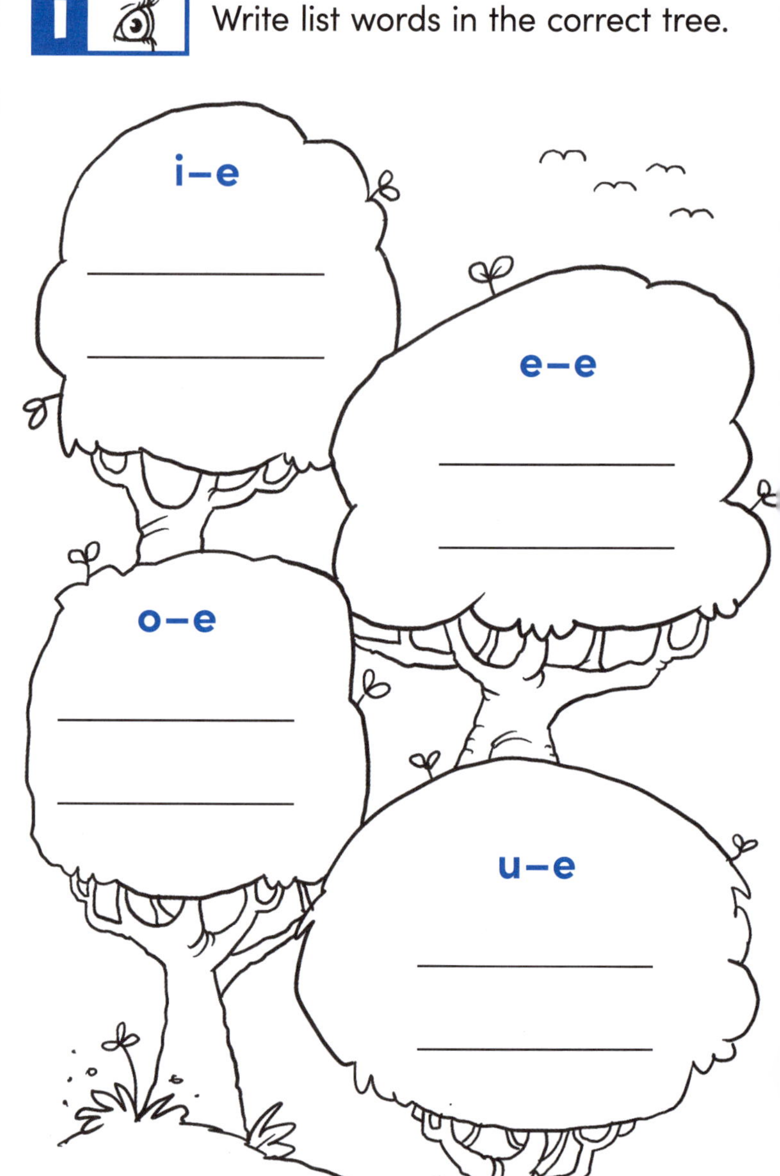

2 Write the word. Then write it again, adding **e** to change the vowel sound.

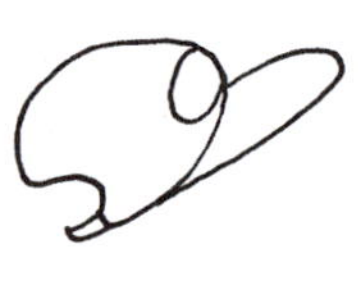

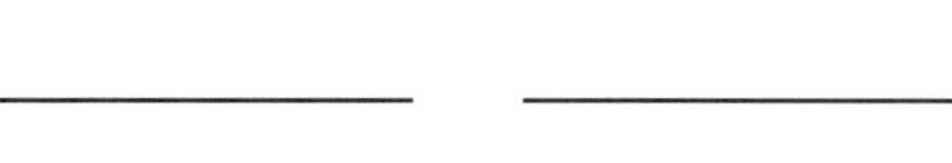

Spelling Rules! Student Book 2 (ISBN 9780655092681) © Janelle Ho, Helen Pearson

 Write two words that begin with the same sound as the picture.

	list word	extra word
	____________	____________
	____________	____________

	list word	extra word
	____________	____________
	____________	____________

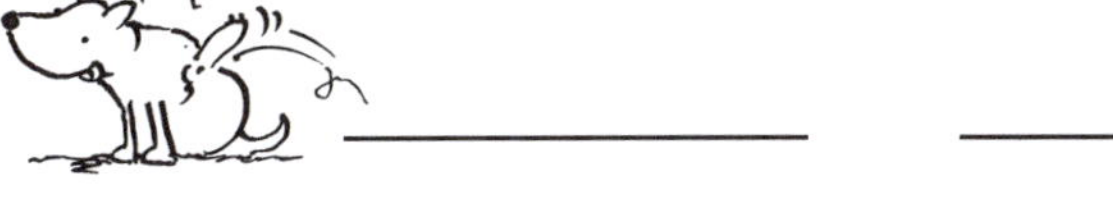

Homophones are words that sound the same, but are spelt differently.

hole = empty space

whole = all of

 Choose the correct homophone.

Shane ate the ____________ cake.

Jane dug a ____________ in the sand.

I tore a ____________ in my pants.

Did you see the ____________ movie?

 Look for small words inside the list word. Write the small words.

place ____________ ____________

whole ____________ ____________

unite ____________ ____________ ____________

Words with a silent **e** drop the **e** before adding **ed** or **ing**.

Smiling, the monkey waved at me.

 Follow the pattern.

plac~~e~~ + **ed** = **placed**

place + **ing** = **placing**

unit~~e~~ + **ed** = ____________

unit~~e~~ + **ing** = ____________

rul~~e~~ + **ed** = ____________

rul~~e~~ + **ing** = ____________

squeez~~e~~ + **ed** = ____________

squeez~~e~~ + **ing** = ____________

Reflection

 I can do this.

 I am not sure.

 I need help.

Unit 3

Say Listen Look Understand Remember Practise	
beg	______
scan	______
clap	______
strap	______
swim	______
begin	______
block	______
throb	______
thud	______
scrub	______
My own words	
______	______
______	______

1 Write the vowels in the first column. Then write words with short and long vowels to fill in the spaces.

vowels	short sound	long sound
a	mad	______
____	______	Pete
____	______	slide
____	hop	______
____	______	huge

Rule If a word has a short vowel sound and ends in a single consonant, double the consonant before adding **ed** or **ing**.

2 Write the word when **ing** is added.

beg ______ strap ______ throb ______

scan ______ begin ______ thud ______

clap ______ scrub ______ block ______

 Circle the pictures that have short vowel sounds.

 Write the missing letter.

beg __ ed	rub __ ed	spot __ ed	plan __ ed
pat __ ed	stop __ ed	skip __ ed	hum __ ed

Most words add **ed** to make the past tense. Some words change. They are called **irregular verbs**. *swim* → *swam*

 Follow the pattern.

swim	sing	stink	begin	drink
swam	s __ ng	st ______	beg ______	________

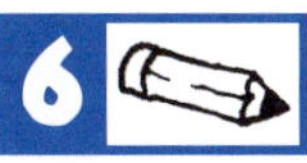 Write a sentence for each word.

thudded ____________________________________

____

____

began ____________________________________

____

____

Reflection

 I can do this.

 I am not sure.

I need help.

Unit 4

Say Listen Look Understand Remember Practise	
lady	______
carry	______
sorry	______
busy	______
pony	______
ready	______
spotty	______
foggy	______
furry	______
chilly	______
My own words	
______	______
______	______

1 Circle the word if the last vowel sound is short, like funny.

crazy cry why daisy

by only sky pretty

Rule

If a word has a short vowel sound, double the last letter before adding **y**.

fun → funny

2 Draw a line between each sound. Underline each syllable. The first one has been done for you.

l / a / d / y　　b u s y

r e a d y　　s o r r y

w o r r y　　h u r r y

3 Double the last letter and then add **y**.

mud ______　　sun ______

fur ______　　bag ______

spot ______

Spelling Rules! Student Book 2 (ISBN 9780655092681)

Drop the final **e** and then add **y**.

ice ______________ choose ______________ flake ______________

wobble ______________ ease ______________ noise ______________

Write a list word for each group. Add another word ending in a short **y** sound.

animals	**people**	**feelings**	**actions**
bunny	aunty	angry	study
______	______	______	______
______	______	______	______

Proofread this story. The story has six words that are incorrect. Circle the mistakes. Then write the correct spelling of the words in the boxes.

Tony's front tooth was wobbley. When it fell out, he lost it. He was not heppy as he planned to put it under his pillow for the tooth fairy. Tony felt silly, but he decided to write a not.

Dear Tooth Fairy,

I am sory I lost my tooth.

Please leave a shinny coin for me.

Tony

In the morning Tony rubed his eyes and felt under his pillow. He found two dollars! Wasn't he lucky?

Change the first letter to make a list word. Which pairs of words do not rhyme?

worry ______________ soggy ______________ beady ______________

Reflection

- I can do this.
- I am not sure.
- I need help.

Unit 5

Say Listen Look Understand Remember Practise	
chicken	___
bucket	___
ticket	___
packet	___
pocket	___
jacket	___
cricket	___
bracket	___
backpack	___
limerick	___
My own words	
___	___
___	___

1 Find a list word for each shape.

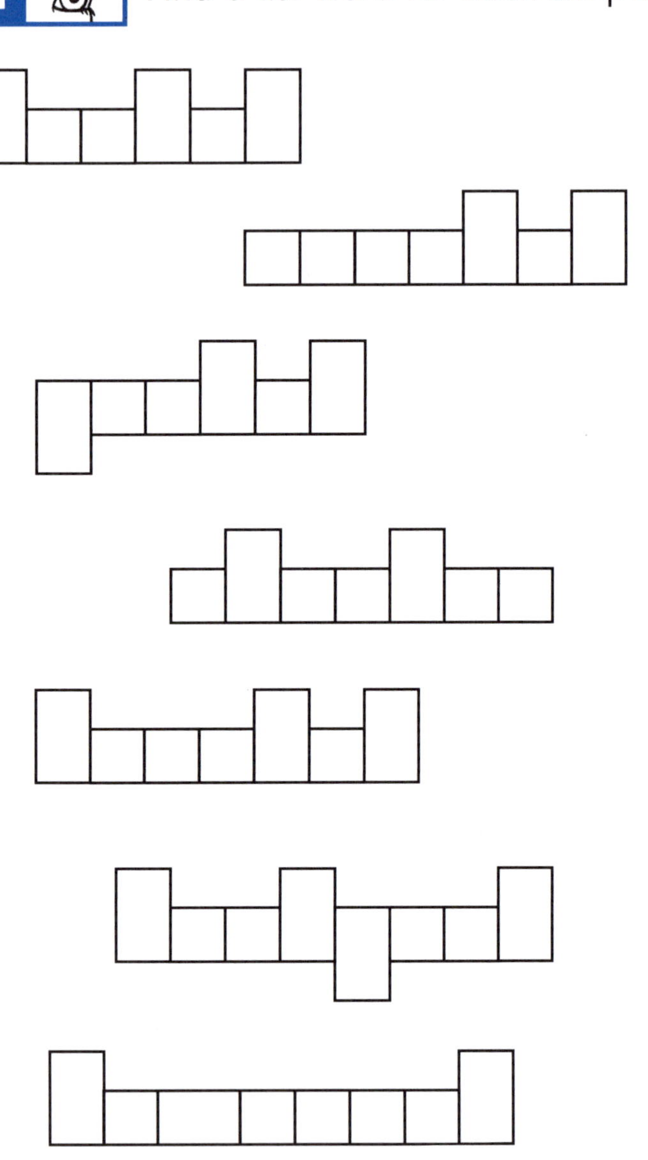

2 Write list words that rhyme.

rocket	wicket	packet
___	___	___
	___	___

Spelling Rules! Student Book 2 (ISBN 9780655092681) © Janelle Ho, Helen Pearson

3 Use the first vowel to put list words in the correct bucket.

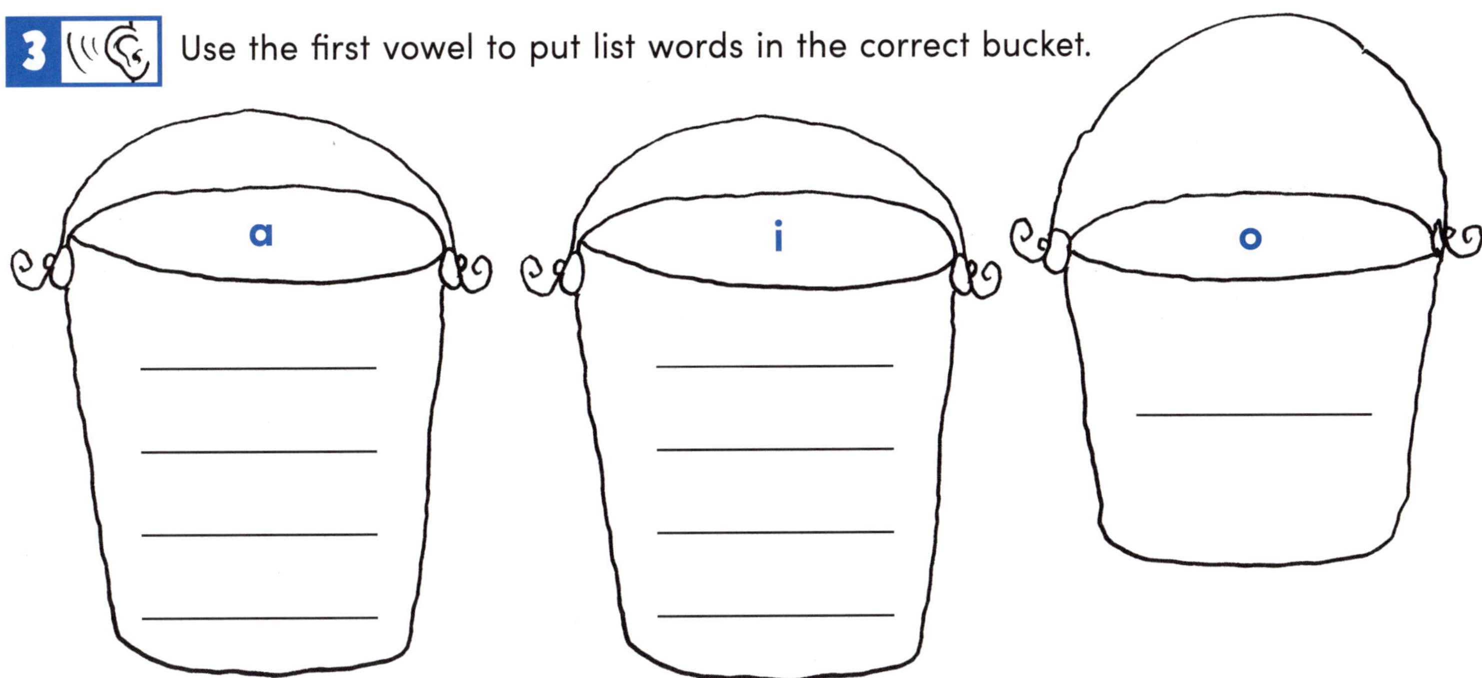

Words that end in **ck** add **ed** to make the past tense.
The number of syllables do not change.

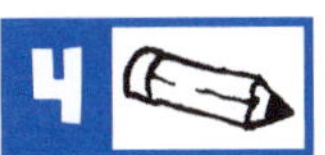

4 Change one letter at a time to make a new word. The first set is done for you.

jacket	packed	locked	packet
packet	______	______	______
pocket	______	______	______
docket	socket	ticket	kicked

5 Say the word. Write the number of syllables in the circle.

sucked ◯	jacket ◯	checked ◯
socket ◯	wicket ◯	pocketed ◯
kicked ◯	bracketed ◯	shocked ◯

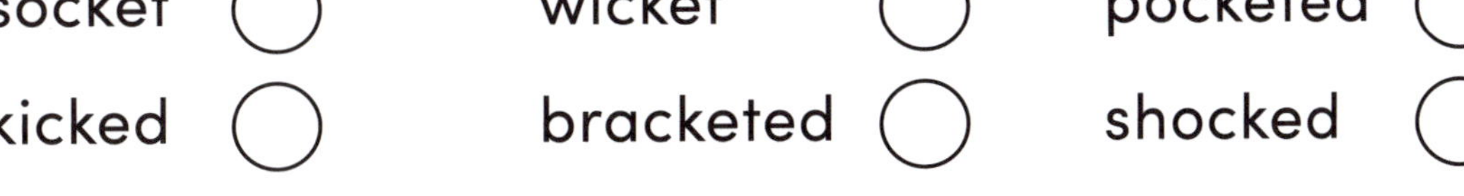

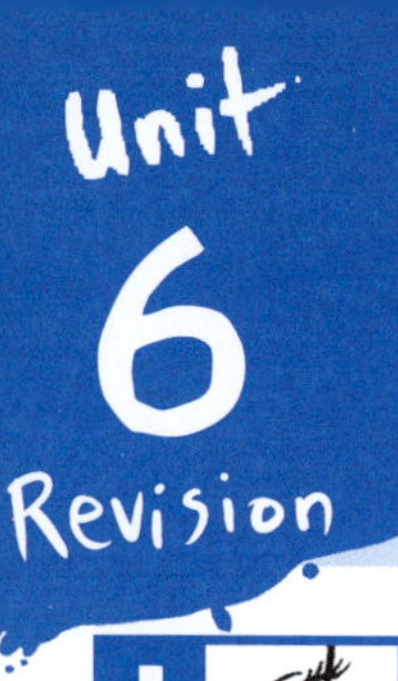

What do you call 10 ducks in a box?

A box of quackers.

1 Write all the words you can see in the word worm.

NEEDSORRYTHERESTOPPEDAREDID

2 Write the words when you add **s**, **ed**, **ing** or **y**. Remember your spelling rules.

	add s	add ed
ask		
rob		
like		

	add ing	add y
puff		
shine		
snap		

3 Say each word. Write in the circle the number of syllables you hear.

kicked ◯ happy ◯ place ◯ begged ◯ needed ◯

finished ◯ pocket ◯ drive ◯ windy ◯

4 Draw lines to match words with the same vowel sounds.

scrape ticket spotty drive steal

cricket steep time rain bossy

Spelling Rules! Student Book 2 (ISBN 9780655092681) © Janelle Ho, Helen Pearson

5 Write the plurals.

three ______________

two ______________

four ______________

6 Look for a small word inside each word. Write the small word.

heel ____________ ready ____________

packet ____________ crowd ____________

fairy ____________ busy ____________

chilly ____________ carry ____________

7 Homophones are words that sound the same but spelt differently. Colour the correct homophone.

Will you come | here | hear | and | meet | meat | my puppy?

Don't let the big dog | steel | steal | the | hole | whole | pie!

Mum will | by | bye | buy | the shoes and socks | two | too |. They will be | cheap | cheep | because there is a | sale | sail |.

8 These words are incomplete. Write two letters that will complete the word on the left and begin the word on the right. The first one is done for you.

sa fe el wi __ __ are the __ __ ady

fir __ __ art sou __ __ em comple __ __ ll

9 Proofread each sentence. Each sentence has one word that is incorrect. Circle the mistake. Then write the correct spelling of the word in the box.

Zac droped his bus ticket on the muddy path. [ ]

Kim packed the cricket kit and is reddy to go. [ ]

Unit 7

Say Listen Look Understand Remember Practise	
knee	______
knife	______
knock	______
lamb	______
thumb	______
wrong	______
wrist	______
listen	______
castle	______
often	______
My own words	
______	______
______	______

1 Say the words and look at the spelling. Circle the silent letters.

knee lamb

wrist listen

knot knock

castle whistle

2 Silent letters are usually part of a letter pattern. Make words with a silent letter.

kn — ife ______
kn — ot ______
kn — ock ______

wr — ong ______
wr — ist ______
wr — eck ______

thu — mb ______
co — mb ______
cru — mb ______

Spelling Rules! Student Book 2 (ISBN 9780655092681) © Janelle Ho, Helen Pearson

Write list words with the same silent letter. Then write a word of your own.

	write	kneel	numb	often
	____	____	____	____
	____	____	____	____
new word	____	____	____	____

Add **s** or **ed**.

Did you know that koalas have thumb___ and knee___?

Before Ken came into the room, he knock___ and listen___ for the teacher to say, 'Come in.'

Write all the words you can see in the word worm.

two-letter words	three-letter words	four-letter words	five-letter words

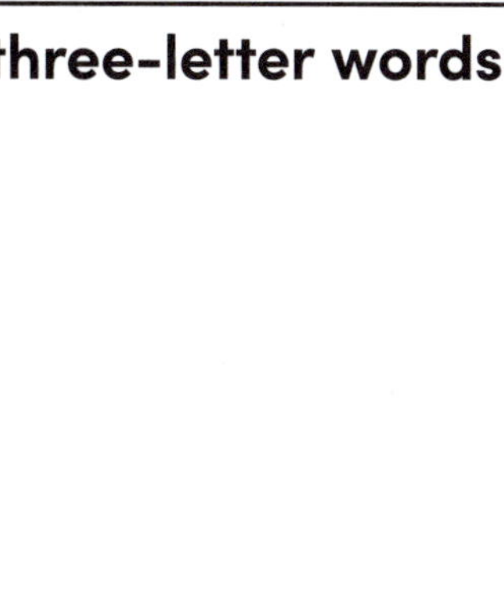

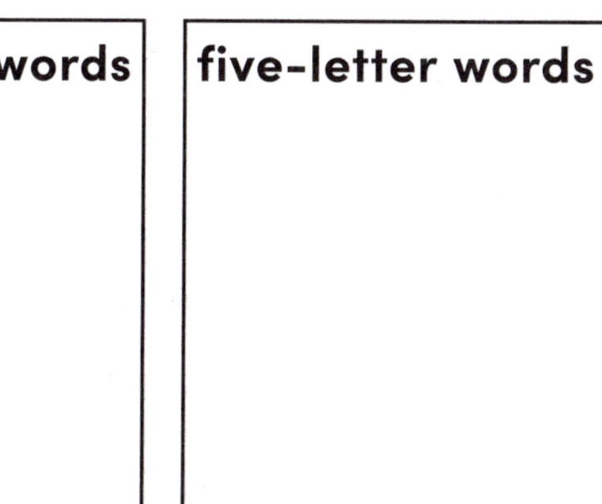

Add a silent letter in each space.

We __nelt to lis__en to the lam__ softly bleating.

The __nob on the cas__le door was the __rong size.

Unit

8

What do you call a skeleton that lies in bed?

Lazy bones.

Say Listen Look Understand Remember Practise	
home	__________
bone	__________
smoke	__________
alone	__________
coat	__________
road	__________
loaf	__________
soap	__________
float	__________
toast	__________
My own words	
__________	__________
__________	__________

1 Circle the pictures with a **long o** sound.

2 Write a list word to match the picture.

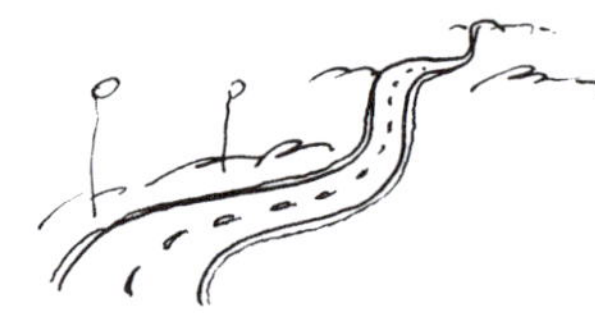

____

____

____

____

3 Write **oa** words.

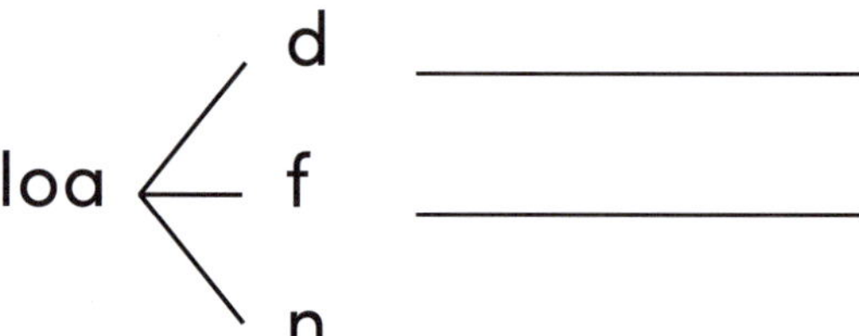

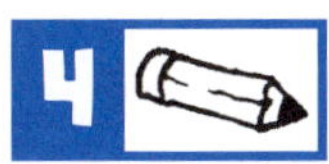

Use the clues to complete the puzzle.

1. Row, row, row your ______.
2. cheese on ______
3. a _____ of bread
4. the place where you live
5. wash your hands with ______
6. be by yourself
7. lie on water
8. something funny

Write the last letter to match the clue.

bigger than a frog	toa__
like a cape	cloa__
a young horse	foa__
sound of a frog	croa__

Add **ed** to the words.

word	add **ed**
soak	__________
doze	__________
toast	__________
joke	__________

Colour the correct homophone.

Joan [road | rode | rowed] a pony and I [road | rode | rowed] a boat.

Why did the chicken cross the [road | rode | rowed]?

Paul has [groan | grown] so much since his birthday.

We [groan | grown] when the player misses the goal.

Unit 9

Say Listen Look Understand Remember Practise	
new	______
knew	______
chew	______
grew	______
blew	______
threw	______
blue	______
true	______
argue	______
cruel	______
My own words	
______	______
______	______

1  Write the words with different first sounds.

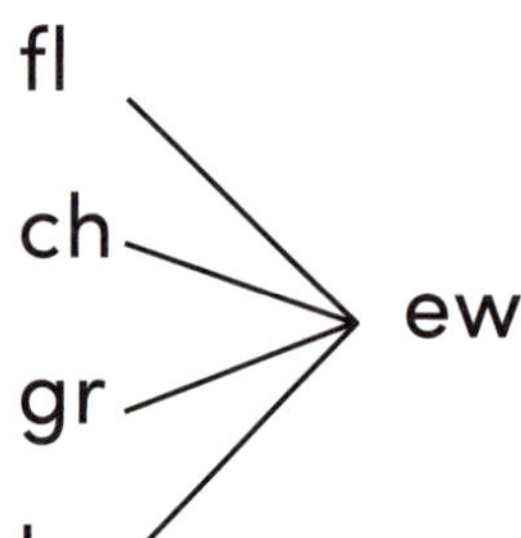

fl, ch, gr, kn → ew

______
______
______
______

bl, tr, gl, cl → ue

______
______
______
______

2 Write new words.

few	glue	grew
~~f~~ → n	~~g~~ → b	~~g~~ → th
______	______	______

3  Say each word. Cross out the words that do not have the same vowel sound as the list words.

moon book do toe four sew

4  Add the last letter to make the word rhyme with **zoo**.

tw__ yo__ sho__ ne__ clu__

5 Choose the best word for each sentence.

The bird flow | flew in the window.

She drew | draw a picture and then throw | threw it on the floor.

When your feet grow | grew it's time for new shoes.

6 Add **ed** to a list word to finish each sentence.

Oh no! My dog has ____________ a hole in Mum's slipper.

We ____________ over who should have the larger slice.

7 There are two pairs of homophones in the spelling list. Write them down.

Pair 1: ____________ Pair 2: ____________

____________ ____________

Now use each homophone once to complete the story.

It was Angela's birthday. She wore a ____________ dress. There were seven ____________ candles on her cake. She ____________ them out as everyone sang 'Happy Birthday!' She ____________ that all the presents on the table were for her.

8 Write the list word with the opposite meaning.

old ____________ agree ____________

false ____________ kind ____________

Spelling Rules! Student Book 2 (ISBN 9780655092681) © Janelle Ho, Helen Pearson

Unit 10

Say Listen Look Understand Remember Practise	
f**ear**	________
h**ear**	________
t**ear**	________
cl**ear**	________
sp**ear**	________
w**ear**y	________
app**ear**	________
d**eer**	________
p**eer**	________
ch**eer**	________
qu**eer**	________
My own words	
________	________
________	________

1 Write the words.

f, h, n, y → ear
____
____
____
____

cl, sp → ear
____
____

d, j, p → eer
____
____
____

ch, qu, st → eer
____
____
____

Colour the circle brown if the word rhymes with **care**. Colour the circle blue if the word rhymes with **here**. Circle the word that can rhyme with both.

pear    dear 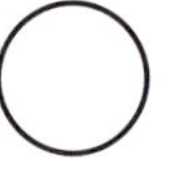   tear ○

fear    wear ○   bear 

Spelling Rules! Student Book 2 (ISBN 9780655092681) © Janelle Ho, Helen Pearson

Words that have the same spelling but different meanings are **homographs**.

tear rip or force apart (rhymes with **care**)

tear a drop of water that falls from your eye (rhymes with **here**)

3 Use a dictionary to write the two meanings of these homographs.

wind 1 ______________________

2 ______________________

bow 1 ______________________

2 ______________________

4 Write the correct homophone on each line.

hear here	Come __________ so you can __________ the music more clearly.
deer dear	The paintings of the __________ are __________ to Dad. They were a present from Grandpa.

5 Write a story using the words in the box.

appear	queer

____

____

____

____

Reflection
I can do this.
I am not sure.
I need help.

Unit 11

Say Listen Look Understand Remember Practise	
reread	______
renew	______
reuse	______
recycle	______
undo	______
untie	______
unkind	______
unfair	______
disagree	______
disappear	______
My own words	
______	______
______	______

re, **un** and **dis** are prefixes. A prefix comes before the base word. When you add a prefix, do not remove any letter.

1 Write the prefix and the base word.

reread = ______ + ______

renew = ______ + ______

reuse = ______ + ______

recycle = ______ + ______

undo = ______ + ______

untie = ______ + ______

unkind = ______ + ______

unfair = ______ + ______

disagree = ______ + ______

disappear = ______ + ______

2 Use the example to write the meaning of each prefix.

If reread means to read again, **re** means ______________.

If unfair means not fair, **un** means ______________.

If disagree means to not agree, **dis** means ______________.

Spelling Rules! Student Book 2 (ISBN 9780655092681) © Janelle Ho, Helen Pearson

3 Add **re**, **un** or **dis**.

____act	____approve	____lucky	____abled
____healthy	____like	____known	____count

4 Write a list word that has a similar meaning.

argue ______________ mean ______________

vanish ______________ one-sided ______________

5 Write a list word to finish each sentence. You may need to add **s**, **ed** or **ing**. Remember your spelling rules!

Pulling a cat's tail is ______________.

I can see the sun ______________ over the horizon.

My little brother has ______________ the laces of all our shoes.

Dad is ______________ the planks from my old bed and building me a desk.

I think we should play tennis but Renn ______________.

6 Write the words with different prefixes. Then write your own sentences using one or more of the words.

un / re > do ____________ ____________

dis / re > appear ______________ ______________

____

____

____

____

Reflection

I can do this.
I am not sure.
I need help.

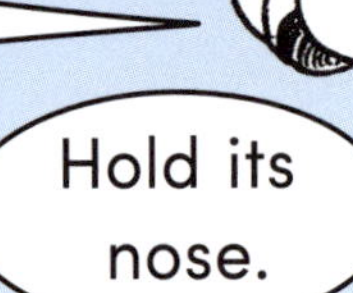

1 Write the verbs when **ed** and **ing** are added.

	add ed	add ing
knock		
appear		

	add ed	add ing
drop		
reuse		

2 Follow the pattern.

blow blew
grow ____________
throw ____________
know ____________

sing sang
ring ____________

sink sank
drink ____________

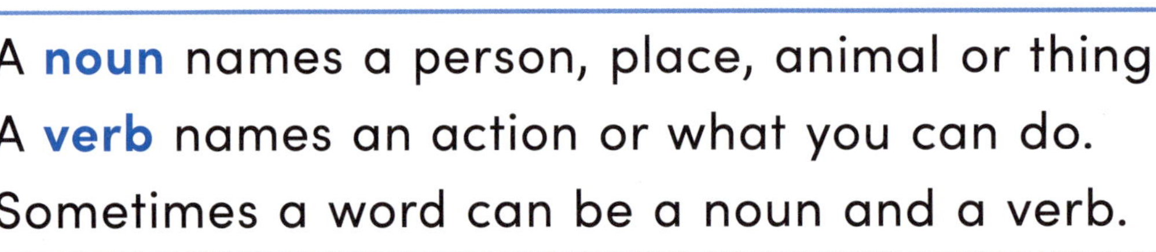

Tip
A **noun** names a person, place, animal or thing.
A **verb** names an action or what you can do.
Sometimes a word can be a noun and a verb.

3 Sort the words into three groups.

blew loaf recycle listen glue wrist year

Noun only
____________ ____________
____

Noun or verb
____

Verb only
____________ ____________
____

Spelling Rules! Student Book 2 (ISBN 9780655092681) © Janelle Ho, Helen Pearson

4 Proofread this story. The story has five words that are incorrect. Circle the mistakes. Then write the correct spelling of the words in the boxes.

Grandpa and I offen go to the swiming pool. Last weekend, the sky was blew but it was cool in the water. We swam till we grew wearie and then we went home. I give the weekend a big thums up!

5 Use the clues to write the word.

The beginning is like	The end is like	The word is
drip	five	__________
clap	hear	__________
cry	numb	__________
start	chew	__________

6 Write other words by following the pattern in question 5.

The beginning is like	The end is like	The word is
__________	__________	__________
__________	__________	__________

Unit 13

Say Listen Look Understand Remember Practise	
sunhat	______
gumboot	______
bedroom	______
shoelace	______
toenail	______
jellyfish	______
raincoat	______
hairbrush	______
newspaper	______
wheelchair	______
My own words	
______	______
______	______

1  Draw a line to join the pictures that make a compound word. Write the word.

______

2 Draw a line to show the two words in the compound word.

starfish schoolbag

earring toenail

armchair toothbrush

3  Write compound words.

bed — room ______ / side ______ / sheet ______

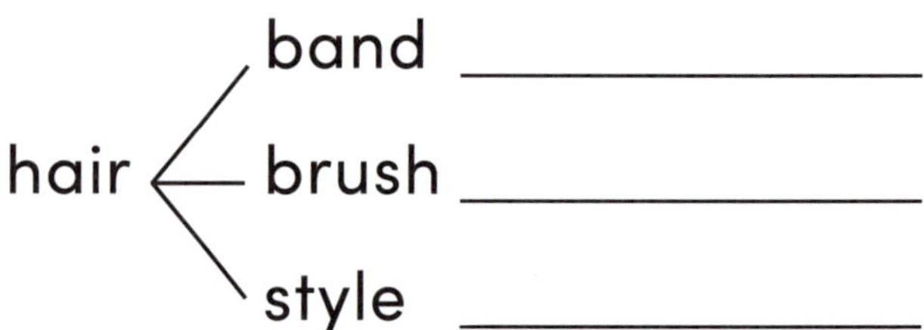

hair — band ______ / brush ______ / style ______

Write the things you see in the bedroom. Draw more items that are compound words. Write these words too.

Draw a line to match the words and make compound words. Each compound word is a body part.

arm jaw finger ear rib belly

button pit cage bone nail lobe

Write the number and word to match each picture.

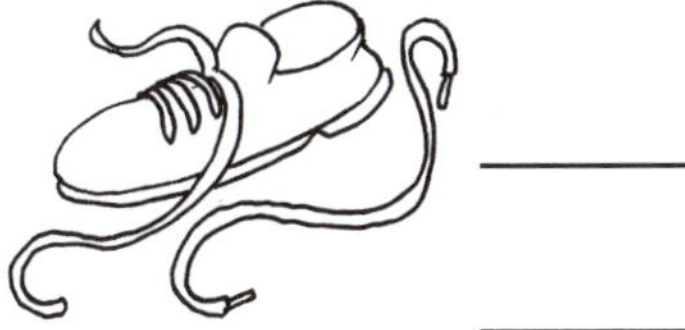

Unit 14

Say Listen Look Understand Remember Practise

bus**es**	______
fox**es**	______
class**es**	______
dress**es**	______
wish**es**	______
brush**es**	______
lunch**es**	______
branch**es**	______
potato**es**	______
tomato**es**	______
My own words	
______	______
______	______

Add **es** to make the plural when the word ends in:

s *buses*
x *foxes*
ss *dresses*
sh *brushes*
ch *lunches*

1  Write the plurals.

noun	plural
bus	______
fox	______
class	______
wish	______
bench	______

2 Write the plural for these nouns.

______

______

______

______

______

3 Write the plural.

sock	____________	hairbrush	____________
dress	____________	lunchbox	____________
plate	____________	branch	____________
house	____________	text	____________

Rule

Add **es** to make the plural when **o** is the last letter and it follows a consonant.

*potato → potato**es***

4 Write the plural.

one tomato, two ____________

one volcano, two ____________

Scratch
Scratch

5 Use a list word to finish each sentence.

When it rains, the children eat their ____________ inside.

Only pick the ____________ when they are ripe!

I like mashed ____________ with gravy for dinner.

6 Imagine you have three wishes. Write what you would wish for.

____

____

____

____

____

Reflection

I can do this.

I am not sure.

I need help.

Unit 15

Say Listen Look Understand Remember Practise	
fish	______
deer	______
sheep	______
mice	______
feet	______
teeth	______
geese	______
children	______
women	______
people	______
My own words	
______	______
______	______

Tip Some nouns do not change when they are plural.

1 Write the singular or plural.

one ______ two fish

one deer two ______

one sheep two ______

Tip Some nouns change when they are plural.
tooth → teeth

2 Fill in the missing letters to show the plural word.

g__ __se m__ce f__ __t wom__n p__ __ple

3 Fill in the missing letters to show the singular word in question 2.

g__ __se m__ __se f__ __t wom__n p__ __son

Spelling Rules! Student Book 2 (ISBN 9780655092681) © Janelle Ho, Helen Pearson

4 Use a list word in each space.

Cats chase rats and __________ whenever they see them.

At the farm I saw __________ , __________ and __________.

__________ pay half price for movie tickets.

5 Fill in the missing vowels.

Ther__ are tw__ w__m__n, thre__ m__n and four ch__ldr__n on the b__s. H__w m__ny f__ __t __re th__re? (D__n't forg__t the driv__r!)

Answer: __________

6 Draw a line to show the meaning of each homophone.

deer	a shy animal
dear	special or not cheap

7 Choose the correct homophone.

Only male __________ have antlers.

Mohan drank water because the other drinks were too __________.

__________ Mr Chan,

Mike was away yesterday because he was sick.

From Sue Lee

Reflection

- I can do this.
- I am not sure.
- I need help.

Unit 16

Why was the **str**awberry worried?

Because she was in a jam.

Say Listen Look Understand Remember Practise	
stamp	______
stew	______
storm	______
style	______
street	______
strong	______
stroll	______
stripe	______
squeak	______
square	______
My own words	
______	______
______	______

1 Circle in green the words beginning with **st**. Circle in blue the words beginning with **str**.

2 Add **squ**.

_ _ _eak _ _ _ash

_ _ _eal _ _ _id

_ _ _ish

Which word sounds like what it is describing?

____

3 Choose the correct word.

An old [steam | stream] train is very noisy.

Dad [stuck | struck] a match to light the fire.

There's a grass [stain | strain] on the knee of my pants.

Flick out the [sting | string] if you are [sting | stung] by a bee.

Spelling Rules! Student Book 2 (ISBN 9780655092681) © Janelle Ho, Helen Pearson

4 Add two letters at a time to make a new word.

in

__in __

__ __ __in __

am

__ __am

__ __ __ __am

5 Choose the correct homophone.

steel = metal

steal = take from someone

It is wrong to __________.

A magnet picks up __________ pins.

6 These words describe different ways of walking. Match the word to its meaning.

stamp	crush with your foot
stomp	walk slowly, taking your time
stroll	beat with force using your foot
stride	walk with long steps

Which two words have a similar meaning? __________ __________

7 There is something wrong with the story. Write a rhyming word beginning with **st** or **str** to make sense of the story.

There is a __________ (play) dog that hangs around our __________ (feet).

Sometimes we throw a __________ (brick) for it to catch. If you don't look

after your lunch, the dog will __________ (peel) it.

It likes chewing on bones but it

doesn't like __________ (pale) bread!

Reflection

I can do this.

I am not sure.

I need help.

Unit 17

Say Listen Look Understand Remember Practise	
itchy	______
witch	______
stitch	______
catch	______
hatch	______
watch	______
fetch	______
stretch	______
clutch	______
kitchen	______
My own words	
______	______
______	______

1 Write words with different first sounds.

w, d, st → itch ______ ______ ______

f, str, wr → etch ______ ______ ______

c, m, h → atch ______ ______ ______

2 Write words with different vowel sounds.

______

______

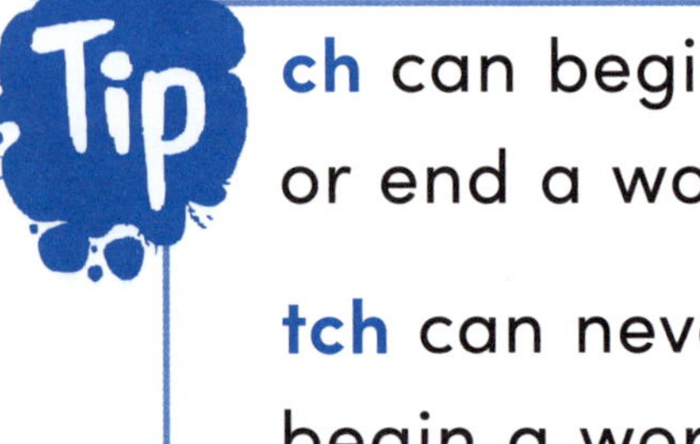

ch can begin or end a word.

tch can never begin a word.

3 Write **ch** or **tch**.

swi ______   ______ icken

______ ur ______   wi ______

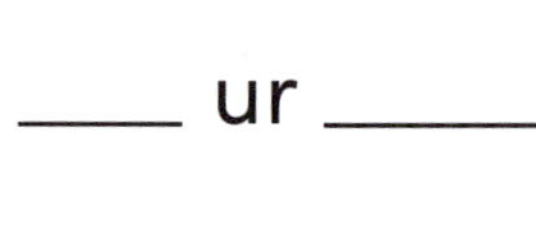

Spelling Rules! Student Book 2 (ISBN 9780655092681) © Janelle Ho, Helen Pearson

4 Use list words to complete the crossword puzzle.

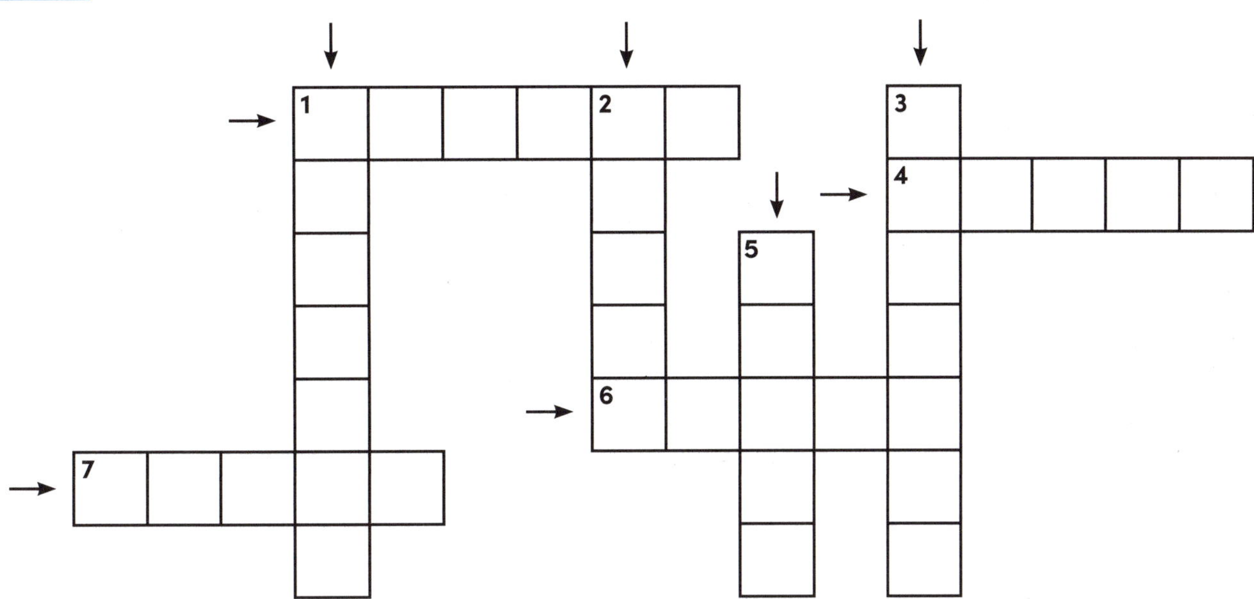

Across →

1. A ____ in time saves nine.
4. The bite on my hand is ____.
6. When will the egg ____?
7. My dog likes to ____ sticks.

Down ↓

1. Always ____ before you exercise.
2. ____ the ball!
3. Dad is cooking in the ____.
5. A ____ rides on a broom.

Write the right word.

witch = a woman who casts spells

which = asks for a particular one

A __________ turned my watch into a clock.

__________ switch turns on the porch light?

Words ending in **tch** add **es** to make the plural.

Write the plural.

match __________

watch __________

patch __________

Reflection

- I can do this.
- I am not sure.
- I need help.

Unit 18 Revision

1 Write the plural.

one coat, two ____________

one plane, two ____________

one child, two ____________

one witch, two ____________

one stripe, two ____________

one tomato, two ____________

one jellyfish, two ____________

2 Draw a line to join up the words that have the same middle sound.

toss	hutch
thumb	stream
grew	bone
road	watch
geese	blue

3 If the letters show the first sound, tick the left box.
If the letters show the middle sound, tick the middle box.
If the letters show the last sound, tick the right box.

ch ☐☐☐

i ☐☐☐

th ☐☐☐

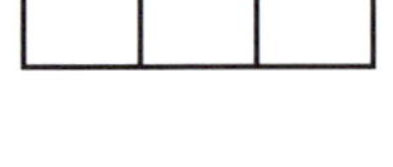

ck ☐☐☐

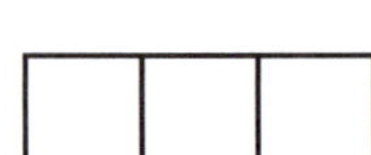

sh ☐☐☐

y ☐☐☐

st ☐☐☐

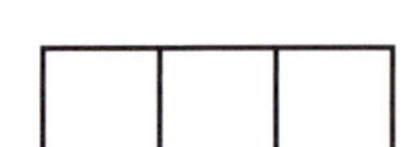

str ☐☐☐

4 Write the words for the pictures. Circle the silent letter.

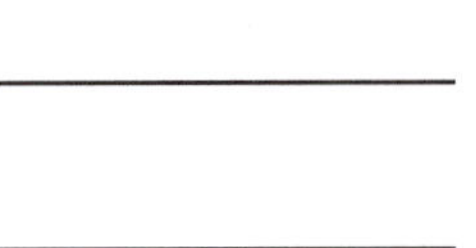

____

____

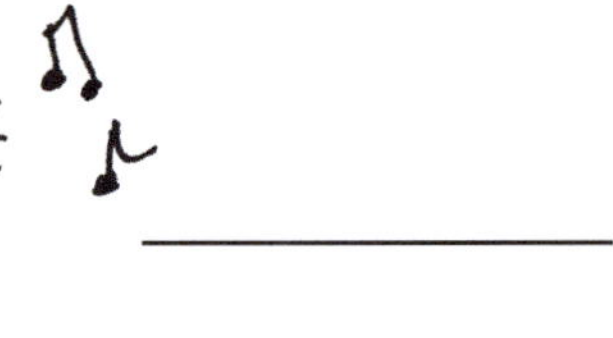

____

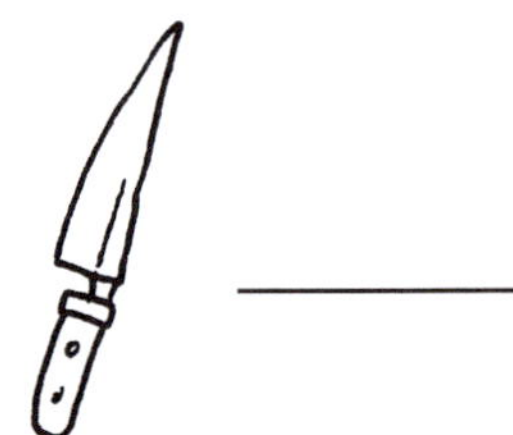

____

Spelling Rules! Student Book 2 (ISBN 9780655092681) © Janelle Ho, Helen Pearson

5 Write the past tense.

stay	stayed
wish	___________
strip	___________
like	___________
chew	___________
appear	___________
watch	___________

6 Add **ing**.

rain	raining
drive	___________
walk	___________
stop	___________
run	___________
wake	___________
stretch	___________

7 Write the irregular past tense verb.

sing	is	blow	drink	do
___________	___________	___________	___________	___________

8 Proofread this story. The story has five words that are incorrect. Circle the mistakes. Then write the correct spelling of the words in the clouds.

It was raining and Tony wanted to visit his granparents. He new his mum would not be happy if he got wet. He put on his raincote and his gumboots. He pickd up the newspaper from the dinning table and went out to the street. Bother! It was not raining anymore.

Unit 19

What do camels carry in the rain?

Humpbrellas.

Say Listen Look Understand Remember Practise	
annoy	________
toyshop	________
join	________
spoil	________
noisy	________
stray	________
delay	________
trail	________
chain	________
explain	________
My own words	
________	________
________	________

1

Write words with different first sounds.

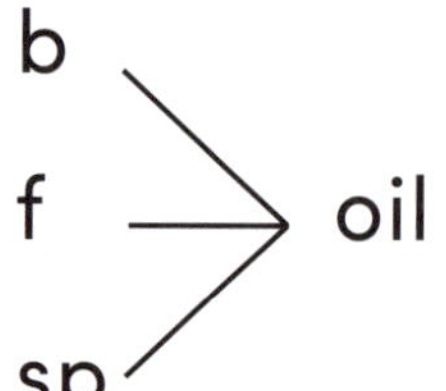

b, f, sp → oil

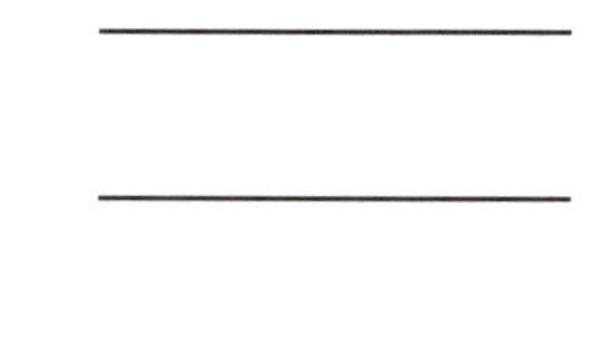

____
____
____

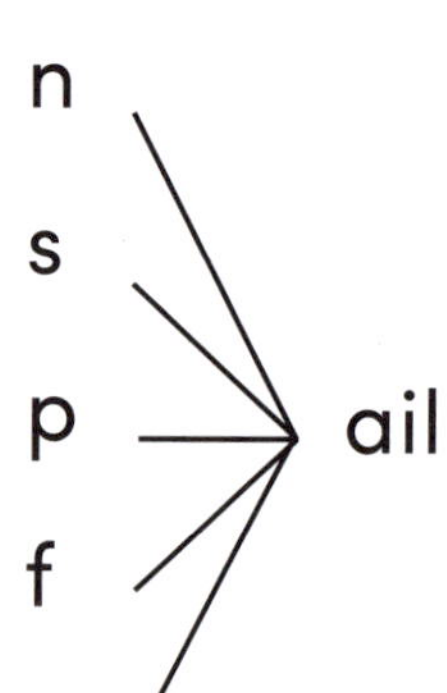

n, s, p, f, tr → ail

____
____
____
____
____

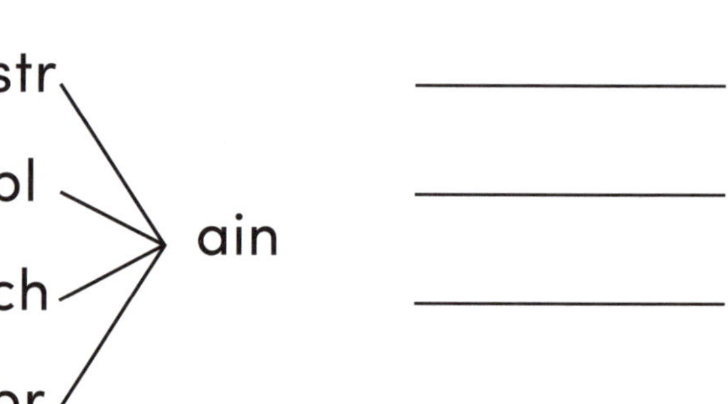

str, pl, ch, br → ain

____
____
____
____

2

Write words with different last sounds.

coi → l, n

____
____

trai → l, n

____
____

3

Remove one or two letters to make a smaller word.

snail	spoil	trail	enjoy	joint	delay
________	________	________	________	________	________

Spelling Rules! Student Book 2 (ISBN 9780655092681) © Janelle Ho, Helen Pearson

oy sounds the same as **oi**.

ay sounds the same as **ai**.

A syllable with **oi** or **ai** must always end in a consonant.

boy	*boil*	*say*	*sail*
toy	*toil*	*ray*	*rain*
joy	*join*	*way*	*wait*

 Fill in **oy** or **oi** to show the vowel sound.

t__ __ box

t__ __let

 Fill in **ay** or **ai** to show the vowel sound.

tr__ __

sn__ __l

tr__ __l

 Write a list word to match each shape.

You should 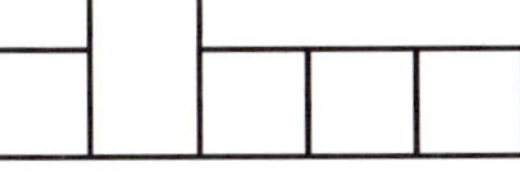 up your bike so it won't be stolen.

The band is so ______, it will 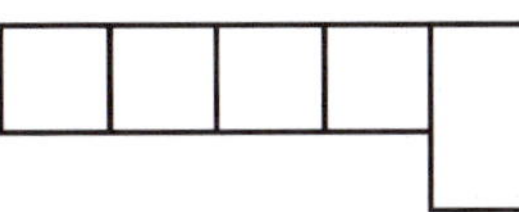 Granny.

Can you 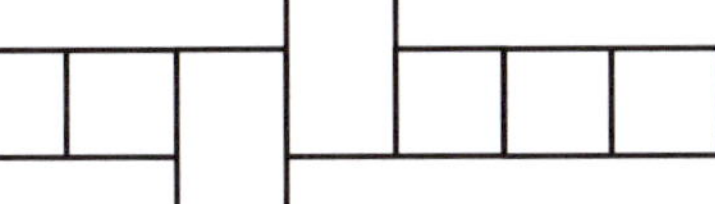 why there is a 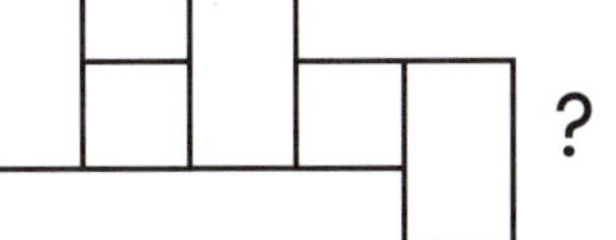 ?

Why don't you 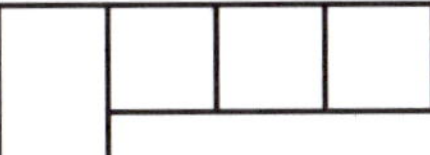 in the game of cricket?

Take your rubbish with you so it won't ______ the park 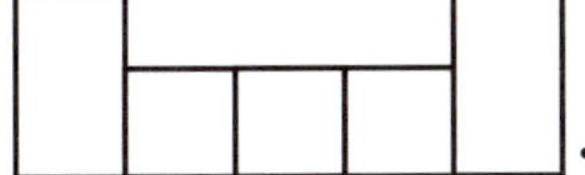.

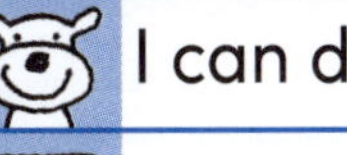 I can do this.

 I am not sure.

 I need help.

Spelling Rules! Student Book 2 (ISBN 9780655092681) © Janelle Ho, Helen Pearson

Unit 20

Say Listen Look Understand Remember Practise	
chief	______
thief	______
field	______
shield	______
piece	______
believe	______
key	______
honey	______
monkey	______
turkey	______
My own words	
______	______
______	______

1 Circle the picture if the word has a long **e** sound.

2 Write the missing letters.

p__ __ce

donk__ __

sh__ __d

th__ __f

turk__ __

monk__ __

3 Which **key** words finish these sentences? They are all animals

We often eat roast ________________ at Christmas.

A ________________ has bigger ears than a horse.

I like to play on the ________________ bars at school.

Spelling Rules! Student Book 2 (ISBN 9780655092681) © Janelle Ho, Helen Pearson

4 Draw a line between each sound.

k e y   p i e c e   c h i e f   f i e l d

t u r k e y   h o n e y   b e l i e v e

These words are **homophones**.

piece peace

5 Colour the correct word.

We all wish for world | piece | peace |.

I also wish for a | piece | peace | of cake!

6 Look for a small word in each list word.
Write the small word.

thief ________   shield ________   piece ________

honey ________   believe ________ ________

7 Colour the correct word.

| Monkey | Monkeys | are some of the cleverest animals in the world.

Some tribes have | chief | chiefs |, but Aboriginal | Mob | Mobs | have elders.

Dad will meet me at the first | field | fields |.

Mum has five | key | keys | on her key ring.

8 There is a list word that is a verb only. Write the word.

____

Unit 21

Say Listen Look Understand Remember Practise	
babies	______
ladies	______
ponies	______
stories	______
puppies	______
cries	______
carries	______
worries	______
hurries	______
replies	______
My own words	
______	______
______	______

1 Write the plural.

one baby, two ______

one lady, two ______

one puppy, two ______

one jelly, two ______

one fairy, two ______

one pony, two ______

2 Write the correct verb.

I carry, he ______

I hurry, she ______

You cry, he ______

I fly, she ______

You worry, Jo ______

Rule

When a word ends in a consonant followed by **y**, change **y** to **i**, then add **es**.

baby → babies

cry → cries

When a word ends in a vowel followed by **y**, add **s** only.

day → days

enjoy → enjoys

key → keys

Spelling Rules! Student Book 2 (ISBN 9780655092681) © Janelle Ho, Helen Pearson

3 Write the base word.

________	→	ponies	________	→	worries
________	→	lollies	________	→	dries
________	→	daisies	________	→	carries
________	→	turkeys	________	→	enjoys

4 Colour the correct word.

The | monkies | monkeys | like to play hide-and-seek.

The girls dressed up as | fairies | fairys | for the party.

Stay away from | bullies | bullys | in the playground.

Our class is writing | stories | storys | set in space.

Rule

To add **ed** to a word that ends in a consonant followed by **y**, change **y** to **i**. *cry → cried*

To add **ed** to a word that ends in a vowel followed by **y**, add **ed** only. *stay → stayed*

5 Add **ed**.

The boys ________ (carry) the boxes and ________ (hurry) into the hall.

Sally ________ (replay) meeting her hero over and over in her head.

'Yes, I'll bring the lollies,' Johnny ________ (reply).

Reflection

- I can do this.
- I am not sure.
- I need help.

Unit 22

Say Listen Look Understand Remember Practise	
saw	___
draw	___
claw	___
straw	___
crawl	___
yawn	___
prawn	___
poor	___
door	___
floor	___
My own words	
___	___
___	___

1 Write words with different first sounds.

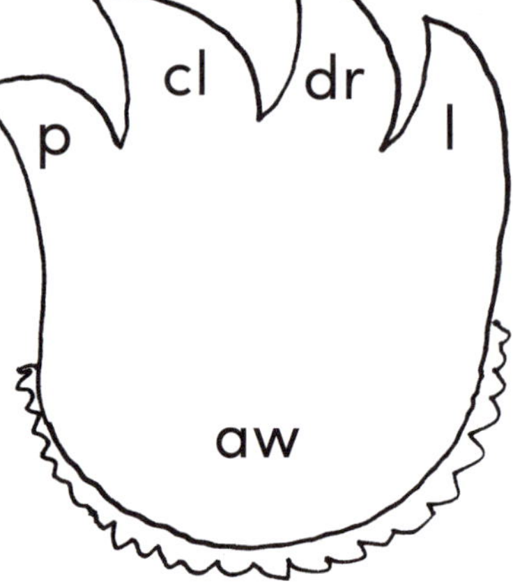

___
___
___
___

2 Circle the pictures with the same vowel sound as saw.

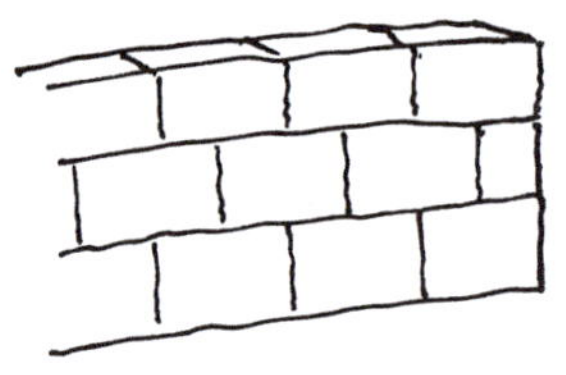

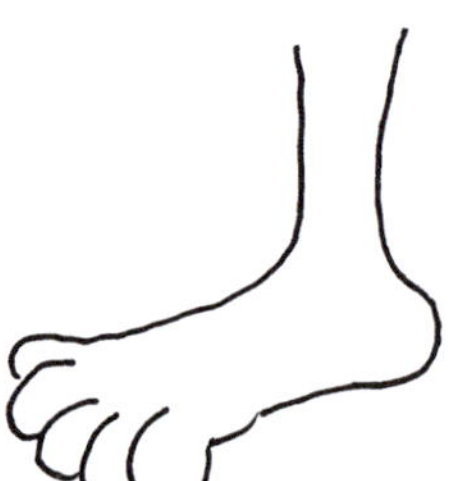

3 aw can be followed by a consonant. Write the words.

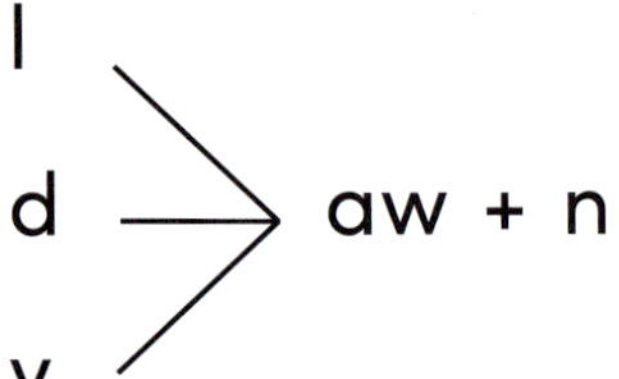

___
___
___

cr
sh
dr
aw + l

___
___
___

Spelling Rules! Student Book 2 (ISBN 9780655092681) © Janelle Ho, Helen Pearson

4 Say each word aloud. Circle the word if it makes the same vowel sound as **aw**.

coast	blood	door	school	shore	roar
broom	four	more	for	floor	how

5 The same sound can be spelt in different ways.
Write a word for each letter pattern that makes the **aw** sound.

aw as in straw and yawn

oor as in door and __________

or as in or and __________

our as in pour and __________

ore as in shore and __________

oar as in oar and __________

6 Draw a line to show the meaning for each homophone.

sore saw	hurting looked at	paw poor pour	not rich tip out of a jug an animal's foot
raw roar	loud sound not cooked	draw drawer	sketch a picture place to put things

7 Colour the correct homophone.

The paw | poor | pour dog has hurt its paw | poor | pour.

A dog with a saw | sore leg is sitting in a draw | drawer.

Lions raw | roar when they smell raw | roar meat.

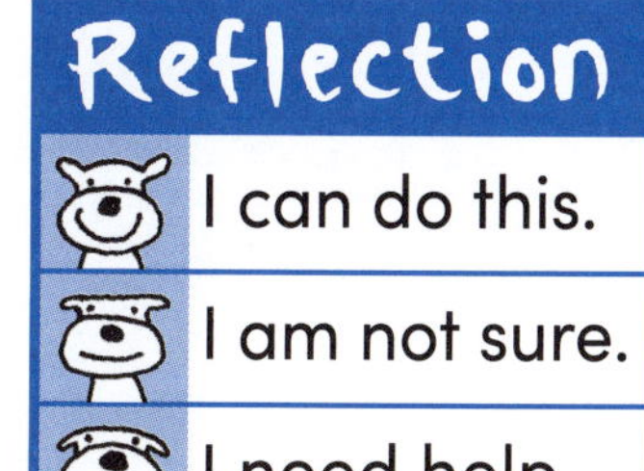

Unit 23

Say Listen Look Understand Remember Practise	
spring	______
sprawl	______
screen	______
scratch	______
split	______
splash	______
shrink	______
shrill	______
throw	______
thread	______
My own words	
______	______
______	______

1 Write the missing consonants.

s__ __ash

__ __read

__ __row

__ __ray

s__ __ing

s__ __atch

__c__ew

s__ __it

2 One word in each column has a different vowel sound. Circle it.

spray	spring	scream	throw
scratch	shrill	streak	how
splash	strike	thread	show
stamp	split	steal	crow

 You get these words if you take letters out of list words. Write the list word.

catch sing see pit sink

 Take letters out of each word to make new words.

sprawl throw thread shrill splash

5 A year has four seasons: spring, summer, autumn and winter. Name the season in each picture. Then write one word to describe that season.

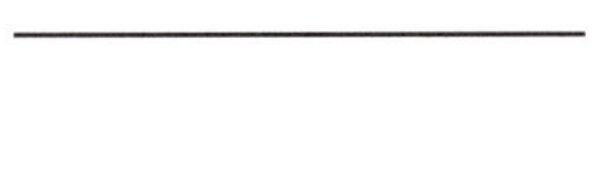

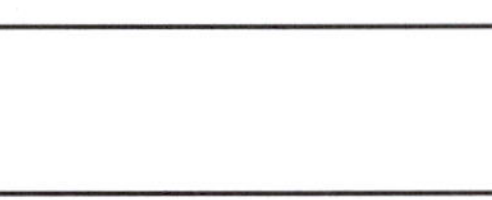

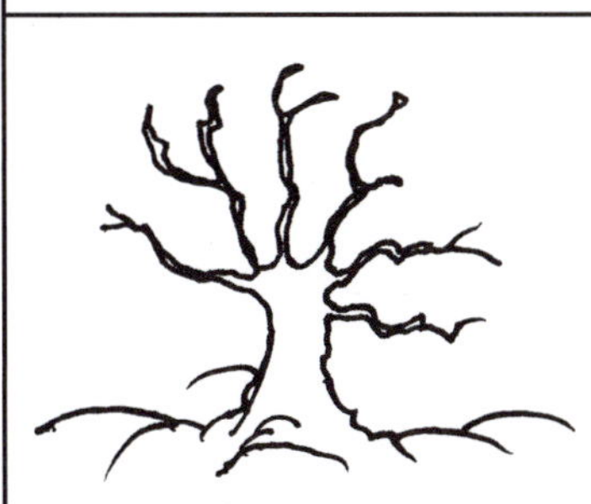

Which season has a silent letter? ____________

 Use the beginning of the first word and the end of the second word to make a new word.

spring + hint = ____________

three + shrill = ____________

split + winter = ____________

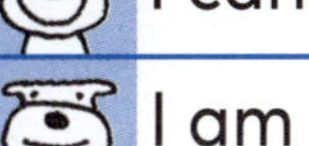 I can do this.

I am not sure.

 I need help.

Spelling Rules! Student Book 2 (ISBN 9780655092681) © Janelle Ho, Helen Pearson

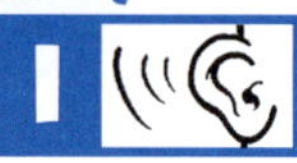 Write the vowels for each word.

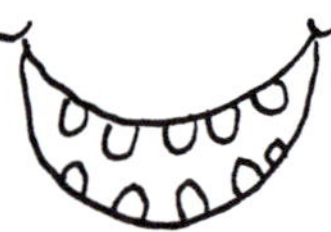
t__ __th

r__ __n

r__ __d

p__ __r

sh__ __ld

b__ __l

pr__ __n

d__ __r

 Each of these words is a homophone.
Write another word with the same sound but different spelling.

saw	hole	steel	new	tale
________	________	________	________	________

 Follow the pattern.

carry is to carries as worry is to __________

wish is to wishes as splash is to __________

shine is to shining as write is to __________

blow is to blew as throw is to __________

step is to stepped as trip is to __________

chew is to chews as draw is to __________

stroke is to stroked as scrape is to __________

boil is to boiling as sail is to __________

4 Write a word you have learnt that matches each clue.

to move on hands and knees ______________

not full ______________

season between winter and summer ______________

someone who steals ______________

you need this to sew ______________

an open space with short grass ______________

5 Write a word to match each clue. Then write some clues of your own.

money + key = ______________

chew + thief = ______________

sport + oil = ______________

__________ + __________ = yawn

__________ + __________ = scream

6 Change one letter at a time to make a new word.

pain	talk
__________	__________
__________	__________
__________	__________
boil	bill

7 What is your favourite season? Explain why. Draw a picture.

____

____

____

____

____

____

Unit 25

Say Listen Look Understand Remember Practise	
I'll	______
he's	______
it's	______
isn't	______
can't	______
don't	______
doesn't	______
didn't	______
won't	______
we're	______
My own words	
______	______
______	______

A **contraction** is the short form of a word or words. Use an **apostrophe** to show that letters have been left out.

I will ⟶ I'll
it is ⟶ it's
do not ⟶ don't

Circle the words that match each short form.

I'm	I can I am I must
he's	he is he was he does
isn't	is not it is does not
can't	care not can I cannot
won't	what is will not what not

2 The window shows which letters must be taken away. Write the short word that comes out of the shrinking machine.

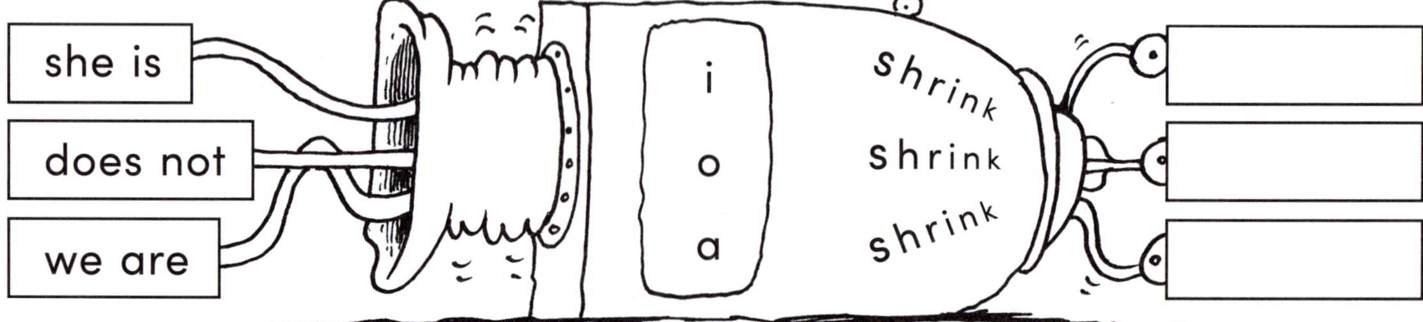

Spelling Rules! Student Book 2 (ISBN 9780655092681) © Janelle Ho, Helen Pearson

3 Write list words to complete the story.

'May I please go to Alex's house, Mum?' I asked. 'No, you ________,' Mum said. '________ Grandad's birthday today and we ________ want to go to his party without a present. So ________ going to the shops now and I need you to help me choose his gift.'

4 **His** and **he's** are often confused. Colour the correct word in each sentence.

Ali packed | his | he's | bag before going to bed.

Don't annoy Annan while | his | he's | working.

5 **They're**, **their** and **there** are often confused. Colour the correct word in each sentence.

| They're | Their | There | are hooks where they can hang wet raincoats.

| They're | Their | There | raincoats were dry by the end of the day.

| They're | Their | There | not allowed to use umbrellas.

6 Write your own sentence using **it's**. Make sure it means **it is**.

____

____

____

Reflection

- I can do this.
- I am not sure.
- I need help.

Unit 26

How does a dentist check a crocodile's teeth?

Say Listen Look Understand Remember Practise	
sadly	________
loudly	________
slowly	________
nicely	________
rudely	________
quickly	________
quietly	________
crossly	________
kindly	________
happily	________
My own words	
________	________
________	________

Adverbs tell us more about verbs.

Adverbs often end in **ly**.

1 Make adverbs by adding **ly**.

ly: proud, soft, sad, quick, strong

____
____
____
____
____

2 Add **ly** to these words.

safe → ________

wrong → ________

unkind → ________

Rule

If the word ends with a short **y**, change **y** to **i** before you add **ly**.

If the word ends with a long **y**, just add **ly**.

3 Follow the rules to add **ly**.

short y	change y to i + ly
pretty	

long y	add ly
shy	

Spelling Rules! Student Book 2 (ISBN 9780655092681) © Janelle Ho, Helen Pearson

4 Use the sound in the base word to group the other list words.

long vowel as in slowly

__________ __________ __________ __________

Which word has a long and a short vowel? qu_ _ _ _ _

5 Write an adverb from the list to go with each verb.

smile	__________	whisper	__________
answer	__________	shout	__________
stroll	__________	grab	__________
run	__________	share	__________

6 Rewrite each sentence using an adverb instead of the underlined words. Don't forget the full stops.

I treated my friend <u>in an unfair way</u>.

____

____

I patted the dog <u>in a kind way</u>.

____

____

Reflection

- I can do this.
- I am not sure.
- I need help.

Unit 27

Say Listen Look Understand Remember Practise	
fern	______
serve	______
person	______
perfect	______
stir	______
shirt	______
first	______
dirty	______
thirsty	______
birthday	______
My own words	
______	______
______	______

1 Circle the pictures with the same vowel sound.

2 Write **er** or **ir**. Use the list words to check.

s __ __ ve

st __ __

sh __ __ t

f __ __ st

d __ __ ty

b __ __ thday

3 Make as many words as you can.

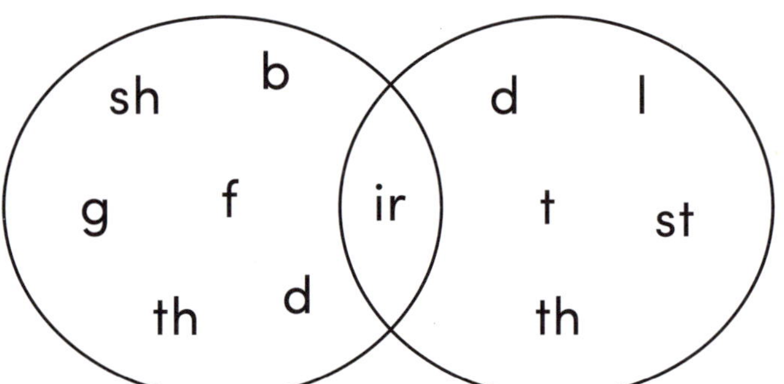

______ ______

______ ______

______ ______

______ ______

Spelling Rules! Student Book 2 (ISBN 9780655092681) © Janelle Ho, Helen Pearson

To compare two things, add **er** to the adjective.
dear → dearer

To compare three or more things, add **est**. *dear → dearest*

You may need to:

- double the last consonant to keep the vowel short
  hot → hottest
- drop the silent **e** *nice → nicest*
- change **y** to **i** *happy → happier, happiest*

4 Add **er** and **est**.

	dirty	safe	quiet	heavy
add **er**	___	___	___	___
add **est**	___	___	___	___

	big	dreamy	short	rare
add **er**	___	___	___	___
add **est**	___	___	___	___

5 Fix these crazy sentences. Write them again using a list word.

I need a drink of water because I am so <u>hungry</u>.

____

Josie scored 10 out of 10, a <u>poor</u> score.

____

Every adult <u>animal</u> is able to vote in an election.

____

Reflection

- I can do this.
- I am not sure.
- I need help.

Unit 28

Say Listen Look Understand Remember Practise	
turn	______
hurt	______
burst	______
nurse	______
curly	______
work	______
worth	______
learn	______
earth	______
search	______
My own words	
______	______
______	______

1 Write words with different first sounds.

b, t, ch → urn

______
______
______

p, n, c → urse

______
______
______

2 Write words with different last sounds.

wor → d, k, m, th, se

______
______
______
______
______

3 Say each word. Circle the words that have a different vowel sound.

word	cure	born	earth	fur
pear	burn	pearl	worm	learn

Spelling Rules! Student Book 2 (ISBN 9780655092681) © Janelle Ho, Helen Pearson

 Use the clues to change Word 1 to Word 2.

Word 1	Clue	Word 2
ear	add two letters	We live on ___________.
curry	change one letter	Her hair is short and ___________.
fork	change one letter	Finish your ___________ quickly!
curl	change two letters	Ouch! I have ___________ my foot.
burn	change one letter and add one letter	Don't ___________ the balloons!
perch	change one letter and add one letter	I had to ___________ my room for my homework.

 Write **ur**, **or** or **ear** words.

Mrs Worthington was surprised to find a ___________ in her ___________.

Gurjit wants to ___________ more about ___________ and other planets.

 Answer the questions in full sentences.

What is your surname? ___________________________

What is your suburb? ___________________________

Use a dictionary to find two list words that do not change in the past tense.

___________ ___________

Unit 29

Why did the orange go to the doctor?

Because it wasn't peeling well.

Say Listen Look Understand Remember Practise	
farmer	________________
leader	________________
baker	________________
teacher	________________
shopper	________________
doctor	________________
actor	________________
visitor	________________
author	________________
sailor	________________
My own words	
________________	________________
________________	________________

er and **or** at the end of a word often names an occupation or a job, or tells you what a person does.

Draw a line to match the word with the picture.

actor

sailor

doctor

teacher

If a word ends in silent **e**, drop the silent **e** before adding **er**.

bake → baker   *drive → driver*

If a word has a short vowel followed by one consonant, double the consonant before adding **er**.

run → runner   *swim → swimmer*

 Sort the words into groups by the spelling rule.

baker jogger manager narrator robber winner

drop silent **e**	double last consonant

 Write a list word to complete each sentence.

I work in a hospital. I am not a nurse. I am a ____________.

I bake bread and rolls. I am a ____________.

I work on a ship. I am a ____________.

I work in the theatre and on television. I am an ____________.

 Complete the information.

author narrator illustrator

The book's ____________ is Hugh Blewett.

The ____________ is Annette N'Post.

Its ____________ is a soccer player.

 Add **er** or **or** to make names of jobs or occupations.

build ____________ inspect ____________

edit ____________ paint ____________

clean ____________ manage ____________

Reflection

I can do this.

I am not sure.

I need help.

Make a word that rhymes.

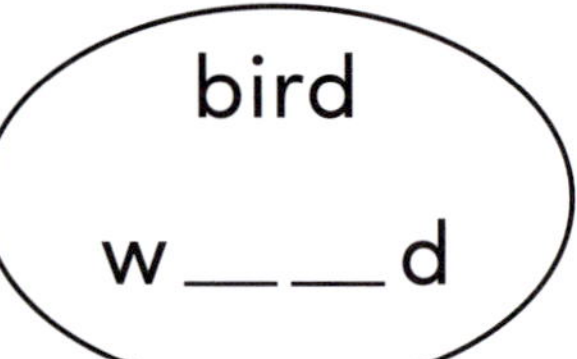

burst

f___st

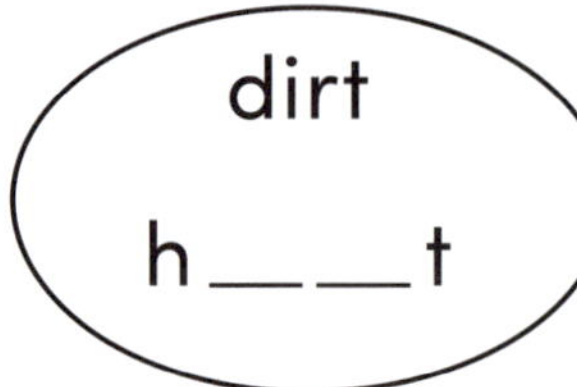

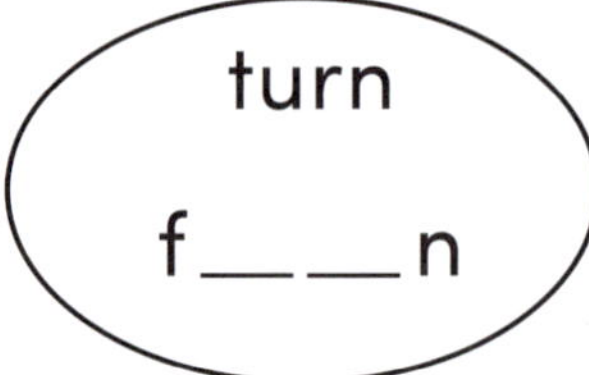

Write the contraction.

I will __________ cannot __________

it is __________ will not __________

is not __________ you are __________

Write the compound word for each picture.

s___f____________

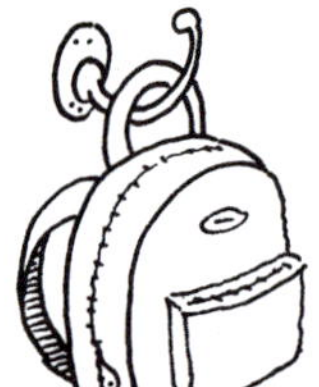

b____p____

______________ch____

er or **or**? Write the correct ending for each word.

act___ visit___ driv___ zookeep___

Add **ly** to each word.

quick → __________ clever → __________

nice → __________ strong → __________

happy → __________ thirsty → __________

Spelling Rules! Student Book 2 (ISBN 9780655092681) © Janelle Ho, Helen Pearson

6 Add **un**, **dis** or **re** to the beginning of each word.

lucky → ______________

tidy → ______________

approve → ______________

dress → ______________

like → ______________

new → ______________

A **prefix** is added to the beginning of a word.
A **suffix** is added to the end of a word.

re, **un** and **dis** are prefixes.

y, **ly**, **ed**, **ing**, **s**, **es**, **er** and **est** are suffixes.

7 Add a prefix and a suffix.

re + do + ing = ______________

______ + kind + ______ = ______________

______ + appear + ______ = ______________

______ + agree + ______ = ______________

8 The text has five words that are incorrect. Circle the mistakes. Then write the correct spelling of the words in the boxes.

In our school garden we grow many flowrs and ferns. We put werms into the soyl and water the plants often. We enjoy geting dirty and waching the plants grow!

Unit 31

What's the best day to visit the beach?

Say Listen Look Understand Remember Practise	
Sunday	______
Monday	______
Tuesday	______
Wednesday	______
Thursday	______
Friday	______
Saturday	______
today	______
tomorrow	______
because	______
My own words	
______	______
______	______

1 The days of the week are often abbreviated. Write the full name for each day.

Fri. ______

Tues. ______

Mon. ______

Sat. ______

Wed. ______

2 Which days start with the same letter?

S ______ T ______

S ______ T ______

3 What day is it?

Today is ______.

Yesterday was ______.

Tomorrow is ______.

4 Look up a calendar for this year and write the day of the week for each celebration.

This year New Year's Day was on ______.

This year Anzac Day was on ______.

This year my birthday is on ______.

NAIDOC Week begins on ______.

FRIDAY 13 JUNE

26 AUGUST

SUNDAY 4 OCTOBER

Spelling Rules! Student Book 2 (ISBN 9780655092681) © Janelle Ho, Helen Pearson

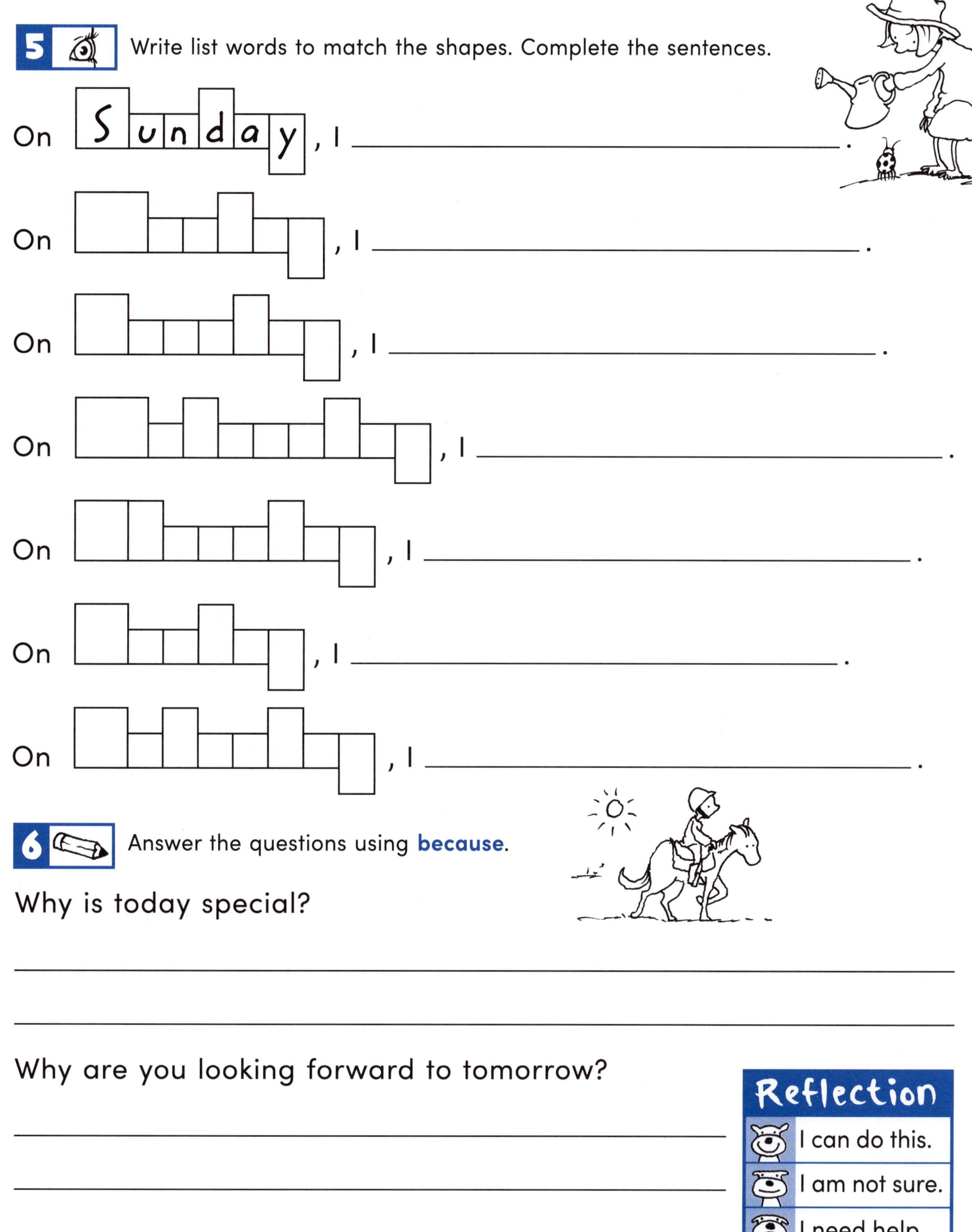

5 Write list words to match the shapes. Complete the sentences.

On Sunday, I ________________________________.

On ______, I ________________________________.

On ______, I ________________________________.

On ______, I ________________________________.

On ______, I ________________________________.

On ______, I ________________________________.

On ______, I ________________________________.

6 Answer the questions using **because**.

Why is today special?

____

____

Why are you looking forward to tomorrow?

____

____

____

Reflection

I can do this.

I am not sure.

I need help.

Unit 32

Say Listen Look Understand Remember Practise	
lie	____________
pie	____________
tie	____________
high	____________
thigh	____________
right	____________
night	____________
flight	____________
height	____________
weight	____________
My own words	
____________	____________
____________	____________

1 Write words with different first sounds.

____
____
____

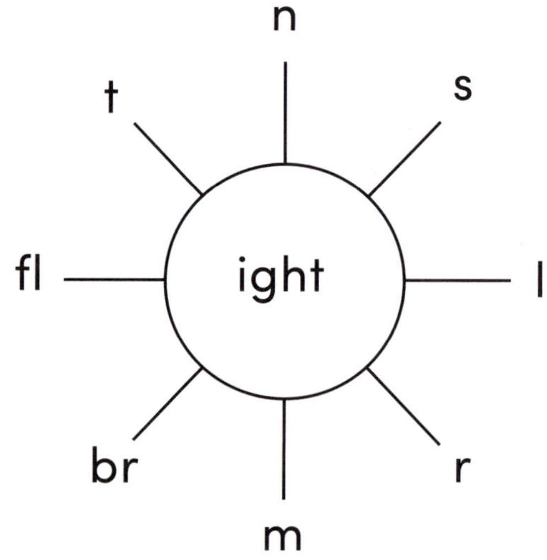

____________ ____________
____________ ____________
____________ ____________
____________ ____________

2 Write a list word.

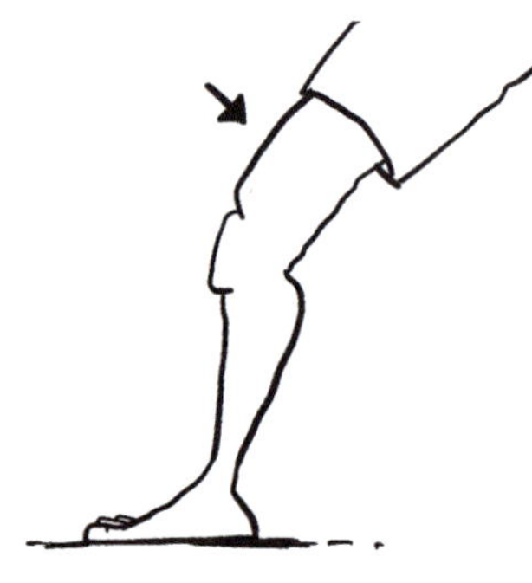

____________ ____________ ____________ ____________

Spelling Rules! Student Book 2 (ISBN 9780655092681)

These words are **homophones**. *piece* *peace*

To remember *piece*, think *A piece of pie.*

3 Write the correct homophone.

This jigsaw puzzle is missing a ______________.

The card said, 'Wishing you ______________ and joy.'

4 Write the name for these parts of your body.

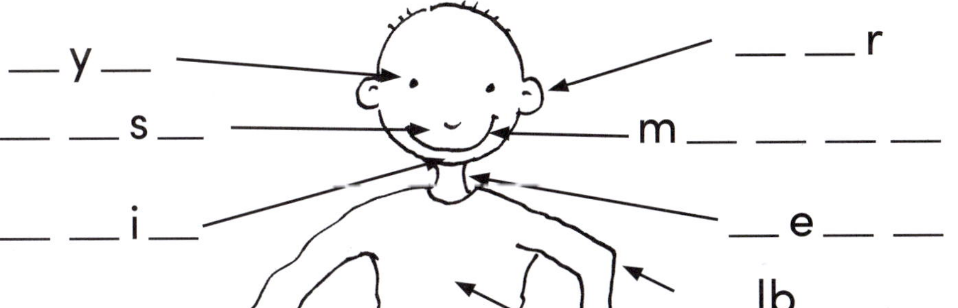

5 Do you know your height and weight?

Height:

I am __ . __ __ metres tall.

Weight:

I weigh ____ kilograms.

6 Complete each sentence with an adjective ending in **est**. You might need to research the answers.

Mount Everest is the ____________ mountain in the world.

Sirius is the ____________ star in Earth's night sky.

Mercury is the ____________ planet to the Sun.

Unit 33

What is the sharpest part of your body?

Your shoulder blades.

Say Listen Look Understand Remember Practise	
build	________
world	________
scold	________
would	________
could	________
should	________
wouldn't	________
mouldy	________
boulder	________
shoulder	________
My own words	
________	________
________	________

1 Find a list word that has the same vowel sound, even though the spelling is different.

________ ________

________ ________

2 Write words with different first sounds. Circle the word with a different vowel sound.

c
w
sh
m
→ ould

____
____
____
____

3 Choose the correct word for each sentence.

would could should

Shh! The band is playing. You ________ be quiet.

Bring your raincoats, as it ________ rain later today.

Kerry ________ rather play outside than tidy her room.

Spelling Rules! Student Book 2 (ISBN 9780655092681) © Janelle Ho, Helen Pearson

Write the contractions for these words.

could not ______________ would not ______________

should not ______________ I would ______________

Add missing letters to match the meaning.

__ __ld	not tame
____ __ld	container to shape a mixture as it dries
____ __ld _	covered with a fungus
__ __ld	heavy, shiny metal
__ __ld	with no hair
__ __ld	past tense of 'sell'
______ __ld __ __	where your arm joins your body
____ __ld	tell someone they've done something wrong

Choose the correct homophone.
boulder = large rock *bolder* = braver or more bold

A large | boulder | bolder | rolled down the mountain in the landslide.

I am shy. My sister is | boulder | bolder | , so she chats with all our neighbours.

7 Write your own sentences to describe the picture.

____

____

____

____

Unit 34

What do you get if you cross a ghost with an elephant?

A big **no**thing.

Say Listen Look Understand Remember Practise	
no one	______
nothing	______
nowhere	______
somebody	______
something	______
anyone	______
anything	______
another	______
everyone	______
everywhere	______
My own words	
______	______
______	______

1 Circle the word with a different first vowel sound.

nobody nothing nowhere

2 Draw a line to show the two words in each compound word.

somebody	everyone
nobody	anywhere
everywhere	nothing
anything	nowhere
somewhere	everything
anyone	sometimes
everybody	somehow

3 Make as many compound words as you can by adding another part.

some ______

______

where ______

______

Spelling Rules! Student Book 2 (ISBN 9780655092681) © Janelle Ho, Helen Pearson

Tip

BEWARE!

no one = two words

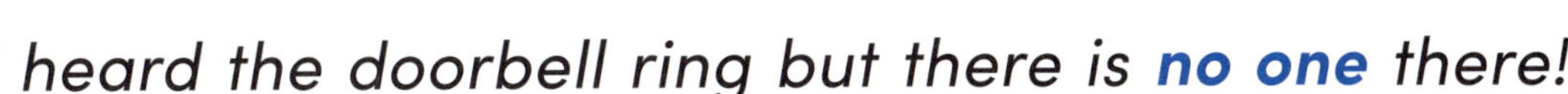

I heard the doorbell ring but there is ***no one*** *there!*

4 Write list words.

Old Mother Hubbard's cupboard is bare.

There is ____________ at all in there!

There is ____________ at the door. I think it's the plumber.

Mum! I can't find my football.

I've looked in the backyard.

I've looked in all the bedrooms.

I've looked ____________.

This glass is cracked. May I have ____________ one?

5 Use a dictionary to help you write these words in alphabetical order.

anywhere anyone anything anybody anyhow anyway

1. ______________ 2. ______________

3. ______________ 4. ______________

5. ______________ 6. ______________

Reflection

I can do this.

I am not sure.

I need help.

 Fill in the missing consonants.

__i__ __e__   __ __a__   __a__ __e__

__ __u__ __   __ __o__e__

 Fill in the missing vowels.

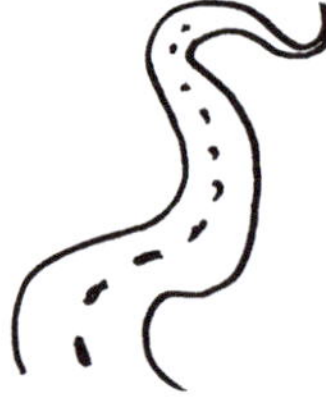

f__rn   gl__ __   r__ __d   ch__ __n   d__ct__r

 Write the noun in the plural.

one joke, two ____________

one hairbrush, two ____________

one class, two ____________

one baby, two ____________

one branch, two ____________

one potato, two ____________

one woman, two ____________

one sheep, two ____________

 Change one letter at a time to make the last word.

give	grew	some	boat
______	______	______	______
______	______	______	______
wire	flow	hops	been

5 This is part of Jing's holiday timetable. What is happening each day?

Mon.		On __________, Jing is ____________________.
Tues.		On __________, Jing is ____________________.
Wed.		On __________, Jing is ____________________.
Thurs.		On __________, Jing is ____________________.
Fri.		On __________, Jing is ____________________.

6 Fill in the missing letters to make rhyming words.

hope	bite	term	reef
s __ __ p	l __ __ __ t	w __ __ m	th __ __ f

7 Write a word that is a homophone. Circle the one that has a silent letter.

paw	seen	stare	for	cent	night
________	________	________	________	________	________

8 Write a verb to complete each sentence.

'I am not!' ____________ Finn angrily.

'I lost my watch,' ____________ Yuki softly.

'Let's go!' ____________ Gita happily.

'Have you been good?' ____________ Santa.

LIST WORDS IN UNIT ORDER

Unit 1
heel
steep
seal
treat
spark
charm
first
third
south
crowd

Unit 2
place
scrape
time
unite
slope
whole
complete
squeeze
rule
cure

Unit 3
beg
scan
clap
strap
swim
begin
block
throb
thud
scrub

Unit 4
lady
carry
sorry
busy
pony
ready
spotty
foggy
furry
chilly

Unit 5
chicken
bucket
ticket
packet
pocket
jacket
cricket
bracket
backpack
limerick

Unit 7
knee
knife
knock
lamb
thumb
wrong
wrist
listen
castle
often

Unit 8
home
bone
smoke
alone
coat
road
loaf
soap
float
toast

Unit 9
new
knew
chew
grew
blew
threw
blue
true
argue
cruel

Unit 10
fear
hear
tear
clear
spear
weary
appear
deer
peer
cheer
queer

Unit 11
reread
renew
reuse
recycle
undo
untie
unkind
unfair
disagree
disappear

Unit 13
sunhat
gumboot
bedroom
shoelace
toenail
jellyfish
raincoat
hairbrush
newspaper
wheelchair

Unit 14
buses
foxes
classes
dresses
wishes
brushes
lunches
branches
potatoes
tomatoes

Unit 15
fish
deer
sheep
mice
feet
teeth
geese
children
women
people

Unit 16
stamp
stew
storm
style
street
strong
stroll
stripe
squeak
square

Unit 17
itchy
witch
stitch
catch
hatch
watch
fetch
stretch
clutch
kitchen

Spelling Rules! Student Book 2 (ISBN 9780655092681) © Janelle Ho, Helen Pearson

Unit 19
annoy
toyshop
join
spoil
noisy
stray
delay
trail
chain
explain

Unit 20
chief
thief
field
shield
piece
believe
key
honey
monkey
turkey

Unit 21
babies
ladies
ponies
stories
puppies
cries
carries
worries
hurries
replies

Unit 22
saw
draw
claw
straw
crawl
yawn
prawn
poor
door
floor

Unit 23
spring
sprawl
screen
scratch
split
splash
shrink
shrill
throw
thread

Unit 25
I'll
he's
it's
isn't
can't
don't
doesn't
didn't
won't
we're

Unit 26
sadly
loudly
slowly
nicely
rudely
quickly
quietly
crossly
kindly
happily

Unit 27
fern
serve
person
perfect
stir
shirt
first
dirty
thirsty
birthday

Unit 28
turn
hurt
burst
nurse
curly
work
worth
learn
earth
search

Unit 29
farmer
leader
baker
teacher
shopper
doctor
actor
visitor
author
sailor

Unit 31
Sunday
Monday
Tuesday
Wednesday
Thursday
Friday
Saturday
today
tomorrow
because

Unit 32
lie
pie
tie
high
thigh
right
night
flight
height
weight

Unit 33
build
world
scold
would
could
should
wouldn't
mouldy
boulder
shoulder

Unit 34
no one
nothing
nowhere
somebody
something
anyone
anything
another
everyone
everywhere

LIST WORDS IN ALPHABETICAL ORDER

actor	Unit 29
alone	Unit 8
annoy	Unit 19
another	Unit 34
anyone	Unit 34
anything	Unit 34
appear	Unit 10
argue	Unit 9
author	Unit 29
babies	Unit 21
backpack	Unit 5
baker	Unit 29
because	Unit 31
bedroom	Unit 13
beg	Unit 3
begin	Unit 3
believe	Unit 20
birthday	Unit 27
blew	Unit 9
block	Unit 3
blue	Unit 9
bone	Unit 8
boulder	Unit 33
bracket	Unit 5
branches	Unit 14
brushes	Unit 14
bucket	Unit 5
build	Unit 33
burst	Unit 28
buses	Unit 14
busy	Unit 4
can't	Unit 25
carries	Unit 21
carry	Unit 4
castle	Unit 7
catch	Unit 17
chain	Unit 19
charm	Unit 1
cheer	Unit 10
chew	Unit 9
chicken	Unit 5
chief	Unit 20
children	Unit 15
chilly	Unit 4
clap	Unit 3
classes	Unit 14
claw	Unit 22
clear	Unit 10
clutch	Unit 17
coat	Unit 8
complete	Unit 2
could	Unit 33
crawl	Unit 22
cricket	Unit 5
cries	Unit 21
crossly	Unit 26
crowd	Unit 1
cruel	Unit 9
cure	Unit 2
curly	Unit 28
deer	Unit 10
delay	Unit 19
didn't	Unit 25
dirty	Unit 27
disagree	Unit 11
disappear	Unit 11
doctor	Unit 29
doesn't	Unit 25
don't	Unit 25
door	Unit 22
draw	Unit 22
dresses	Unit 14
earth	Unit 28
everyone	Unit 34
everywhere	Unit 34
explain	Unit 19
farmer	Unit 29
fear	Unit 10
feet	Unit 15
fern	Unit 27
fetch	Unit 17
field	Unit 20
first	Unit 1
fish	Unit 15
flight	Unit 32
float	Unit 8
floor	Unit 22
foggy	Unit 4
foxes	Unit 14
Friday	Unit 31
furry	Unit 4
geese	Unit 15
grew	Unit 9
gumboot	Unit 13
hairbrush	Unit 13
happily	Unit 26
hatch	Unit 17
hear	Unit 10
heel	Unit 2
height	Unit 32
he's	Unit 25
high	Unit 32
home	Unit 8
honey	Unit 20
hurries	Unit 21
hurt	Unit 28
I'll	Unit 25
isn't	Unit 25
itchy	Unit 17
it's	Unit 25
jacket	Unit 5
jellyfish	Unit 13
join	Unit 19
key	Unit 20
kindly	Unit 26
kitchen	Unit 17
knee	Unit 7
knew	Unit 9
knife	Unit 7
knock	Unit 7
ladies	Unit 21
lady	Unit 4
lamb	Unit 7
leader	Unit 29
learn	Unit 28
lie	Unit 32
limerick	Unit 5
listen	Unit 7
loaf	Unit 8
loudly	Unit 26
lunches	Unit 14
mice	Unit 15
Monday	Unit 31
monkey	Unit 20
mouldy	Unit 33
new	Unit 9
newspaper	Unit 13
nicely	Unit 26
night	Unit 32
noisy	Unit 19
no one	Unit 34
nothing	Unit 34
nowhere	Unit 34
nurse	Unit 28
often	Unit 7
packet	Unit 5
peer	Unit 10

people Unit 15
perfect Unit 27
person Unit 27
pie Unit 32
piece Unit 20
place Unit 2
pocket Unit 5
ponies Unit 21
poor Unit 22
pony Unit 4
potatoes Unit 14
prawn Unit 22
puppies Unit 21

queer Unit 10
quickly Unit 26
quietly Unit 26

raincoat Unit 13
ready Unit 4
recycle Unit 11
renew Unit 11
replies Unit 21
reread Unit 11
reuse Unit 11
right Unit 32
road Unit 8
rudely Unit 26
rule Unit 2

sadly Unit 26
sailor Unit 29
Saturday Unit 31
saw Unit 22
scan Unit 3
scold Unit 33
scrape Unit 2
scratch Unit 23
screen Unit 23
scrub Unit 3
seal Unit 1
search Unit 28
serve Unit 27
sheep Unit 15
shield Unit 20
shirt Unit 27
shoelace Unit 13
shopper Unit 29
should Unit 33
shoulder Unit 33
shrill Unit 23
shrink Unit 23
slope Unit 2
slowly Unit 26
smoke Unit 8
soap Unit 8
somebody Unit 34
something Unit 34
sorry Unit 4
south Unit 1
spark Unit 1
spear Unit 10
splash Unit 23
split Unit 23
spoil Unit 19
spotty Unit 4
sprawl Unit 23
spring Unit 23
square Unit 16
squeak Unit 16
squeeze Unit 2
stamp Unit 16
steep Unit 1
stew Unit 16
stir Unit 27
stitch Unit 17
stories Unit 21
storm Unit 16
strap Unit 3
straw Unit 22
stray Unit 19
street Unit 16
stretch Unit 17
stripe Unit 16
stroll Unit 16
strong Unit 16
style Unit 16
Sunday Unit 31
sunhat Unit 13
swim Unit 3

teacher Unit 29
tear Unit 10
teeth Unit 15
thief Unit 20
thigh Unit 32
third Unit 1
thirsty Unit 27
thread Unit 23
threw Unit 9
throb Unit 3
throw Unit 23
thud Unit 3
thumb Unit 7
Thursday Unit 31
ticket Unit 5
tie Unit 32
time Unit 2
toast Unit 8
today Unit 31
toenail Unit 13
tomatoes Unit 14
tomorrow Unit 31
toyshop Unit 19
trail Unit 19
treat Unit 1
true Unit 9
Tuesday Unit 31
turkey Unit 20
turn Unit 28
undo Unit 11
unfair Unit 11
unite Unit 2
unkind Unit 11
untie Unit 11

visitor Unit 29

watch Unit 17
weary Unit 10
Wednesday Unit 31
weight Unit 32
we're Unit 25
wheelchair Unit 13
whole Unit 2
wishes Unit 14
witch Unit 17
women Unit 15
won't Unit 25
work Unit 28
world Unit 33
worries Unit 21
worth Unit 28
would Unit 33
wouldn't Unit 33
wrist Unit 7
wrong Unit 7

yawn Unit 22

SPELLING RULES AND TIPS

To make a plural

When a word ends in **s**, **x**, **ss**, **sh**, **ch** or **tch**, add **es**.

buses foxes dresses brushes lunches latches

When a word ends in a consonant followed by **o**, add **es**.

potato → potatoes

When a word ends in a consonant followed by **y**, change **y** to **i**, then add **es**.

baby → babies

When a word ends in a vowel followed by **y**, add **s** only.

day → days

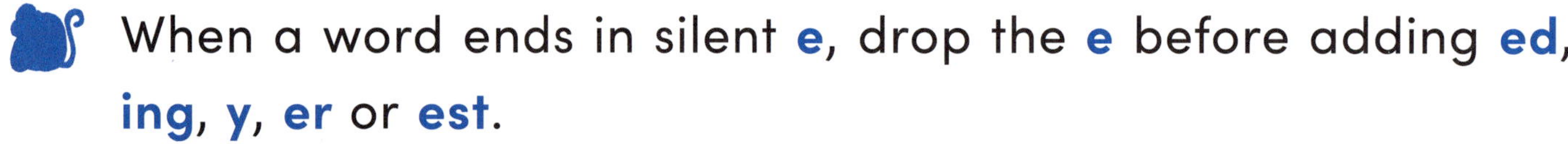

When a word ends in silent **e**, drop the **e** before adding **ed**, **ing**, **y**, **er** or **est**.

smile → smiled care → caring bake → baker

If a word has a short vowel sound, double the last letter before adding **ed**, **ing**, **y**, **er** or **est**.

sun → sunny hot → hotter hot → hottest

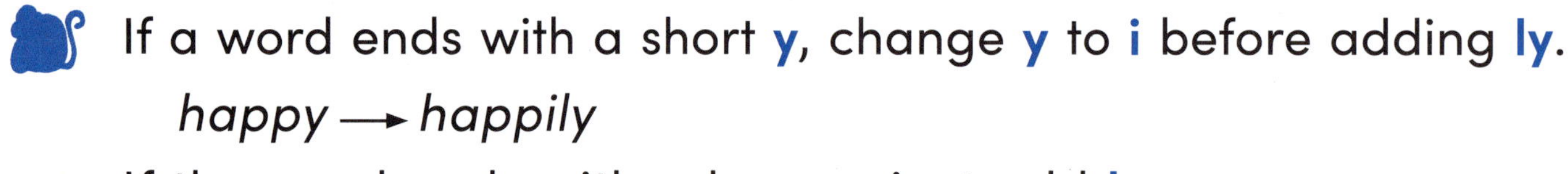

If a word ends with a short **y**, change **y** to **i** before adding **ly**.

happy → happily

If the word ends with a long **y**, just add **ly**.

shy → shyly

A prefix is added to the beginning of a word.

A suffix is added to the end of a word.

re, **un** and **dis** are prefixes.

y, **ly**, **ed**, **ing**, **s**, **es**, **er** and **est** are suffixes.

Spelling Rules! Student Book 2 (ISBN 9780655092681) © Janelle Ho, Helen Pearson